W9-AMK-395

Believing in Senior Living

Insight and Inspiration for the Future of Our Profession

By M. Sloan Bentley
with Daniel Pryfogle

S E N I O R I T Y, I N C.

Copyright © 2011 by Seniority, Inc.
All rights reserved.

For permissions or other inquiries, contact Seniority, Inc. at:
Seniority, Inc.
6120 Stoneridge Mall Road
Third Floor
Pleasanton, CA 94588
925-924-7187
info@seniorityinc.com

To order copies of the book, go to:
http://www.seniorityinc.com

Printed in the United States of America
ISBN: 1466388501

For the gift of grandparents in our lives
For Harry and Violet Thomas

CONTENTS

PREFACE

If ever there was any doubt that senior living is a tough business, there's no question now. The economic turmoil of the past few years simply magnifies the challenges our profession already faces.

How to reposition tired-looking communities? How to compete in a crowded marketplace? How to attract and retain talent? Our clients grapple with such difficult questions daily – even when the economy is strong.

Yet for those who persevere, there's not a business more gratifying. We have the privilege to accompany older adults in the journey of aging. We support their independence. We provide relief to caregivers. We bring peace of mind to families. We do all of this by creating communities known for their hospitality – places known as home.

At Seniority, we are hopeful about our business because we believe in our profession. We know that senior living at its best plays an essential role in the health and vitality of families, neighborhoods, and the nation as a whole. We are optimistic because the need for our services is growing. Indeed, demand will continue to climb as the population ages.

This is the time to be investing in quality people and programs. Seniority is doing just that. We have launched a one-of-a-kind hospitality and culture formation initiative for senior living. Our goal is for everyone to be fully committed and inspired to provide exceptional service in our communities. We call this program Seniority Spirit.

To our clients, friends and colleagues, we say – be encouraged. There are many reasons to be hopeful about our shared work. This book explores some of the challenges senior living professionals face, but the accent is really on opportunity: the possibilities that await all of us who are committed to creating memorable experiences for older adults and their families.

Every day in every Seniority community we start with a special ritual:

The Daily Huddle. For 15 minutes we stand together as colleagues and reinforce our shared commitment to excellence. We explore an educational topic. Then we take a few moments to reacquaint ourselves with our foundational beliefs, such as the mission statement or one of our 14 service commitments. After highlighting team member successes and quickly checking in on the day's agenda, we close with an inspirational quote. We remind each other why we do this work.

Consider this book a huddle of sorts. You might even use it for your own Daily Huddle.

Most of the chapters are quick reads – ideal for brief but valuable reflection, whether reading on your own or with colleagues. The longer chapters that lead off the four sections explore specific issues in greater depth. Every chapter ends with questions for discussion.

You'll find here some helpful "takeaways": analysis of senior living trends, insight on where our profession is headed, and practical advice about steps you can take to create a positive future for your organization. A lot of this advice we've shared in recent years through white papers, presentations, and our e-newsletter *Seniority Connection*. But in this book we spell out more of our thinking and review some of the lessons we've learned, all with the aim of helping other leaders. We hope the book enhances your understanding and increases your skills.

Above all, we hope the book inspires you. We will have offered something valuable if the book increases your confidence in senior living and fires your imagination for the future of our profession.

Introduction

Robert Fulghum's best-selling book has a great title: *All I Really
Need to Know I Learned in Kindergarten.* That statement rings true for
me. All I really need to know, about life in general and senior living in
particular, I learned right around kindergarten in Martins Ferry, Ohio,
and I learned it from my grandfather.

I was extraordinarily close to my grandfather. He was my babysit-
ter, my playmate, and one of the most influential individuals of my
life. He and my grandmother came from large West Virginia farming
families. Neither went to high school or college. They had very little
money. But they were good salt-of-the-earth people. They were hard
workers. And church, family, and friends were extremely important
to them.

My parents' house and my grandparents' house were about a mile
apart. In between was my family's store and wholesale butcher shop
– Bentley's Pick 'N Pack. My grandfather and I would walk from our
houses to the store and back every day. He'd say, "Sloan, let's leave to
get the stink off," and away we'd go with our dog Brownie. The story
was he had to replace the wheels on my buggy every year because of
all of our walking.

Martins Ferry is a front porch town. So on our way back home,
we would often stop and sit on the porches with my grandfather's
friends. They were all retired. Most were coal and steel workers like

1

my grandfather. Many of them were veterans. As you can imagine, I heard lots of stories on those porches.

I was comfortable around older adults. My affinity for seniors, my respect for their service to their country, my pride in being an American – all of that was instilled in Martins Ferry. I didn't know it then, but my walks with my grandfather were preparing me for a career in senior living. I cherish the opportunity to learn from my grandparents and formed my foundational values and belief in people and faith.

The month after I turned six, my mother died of a heart attack at the age of 43. My father was devastated, as was my grandmother. My older siblings were already out of high school by the time I finished kindergarten. So it fell to my grandfather to really raise me. I am forever grateful for his care and his kindness.

When I got to college and started figuring out what I wanted to do with my life, working with older adults seemed like the most natural path to take. Having been in this field since 1987, I know that many colleagues share similar stories – formative stories of influential older family members, of genuine interest in the lives of older adults, of a desire to give back in gratitude. These stories matter. It's why we're here.

There's another story I want to tell now. It's the story of Seniority. I think it's helpful to recount the journey of our firm because the story illustrates the profound changes taking place in our profession.

The initial vision for Seniority sprang from a simple idea: the sales and marketing services of our nonprofit parent organization, ABHOW, had great value. Since 1949 ABHOW has been a pioneering leader in senior housing and health care. We recognized that ABHOW's expertise was so valuable, other organizations would pay for that experience.

The problem? ABHOW would jeopardize its tax-exempt status if it engaged in fee-for-service consulting. However, if ABHOW could create a subsidiary firm to serve its own communities as well as new clients, the tax exemption would be protected and the organization would achieve a double-bottom line: the expansion of the mission and the creation of new revenue to sustain the mission.

In science and technology, they call such solutions "elegant." I call it beautiful.

That was 1997. Bill Clinton was president. The Internet was taking off, and the American economy was booming. It was still several years before the concept of "social enterprise" started to catch on, the idea that a nonprofit could pursue a double-bottom line. We didn't know we were social entrepreneurs. We just saw an opportunity and it simply made sense.

Moreover, our leadership understood that maxim first attributed to the Daughters of Charity: "No margin, no mission." Joe Anderson, Seniority's founding president and one of my mentors, wisely and regularly reminded us that both margin and mission are essential, and that we cannot neglect either.

Our senior living colleagues understood this as well. In later chapters, I'll talk about the growing sophistication of our profession. But hold on to 1997, the year of Seniority's launch. It's a helpful marker for our field. Looking back, I see a sea change from that moment on, as a significant number of senior living organizations that started as ministries truly shifted to a business orientation – in order to do more ministry.

Since 1997 Seniority has grown into one of the nation's most respected senior living management, sales and marketing firms. Along the way, we made ABHOW better. Every year we achieved ABHOW's entrance fee goal, collecting more than $293 million between 1997-2011. We extended ABHOW's mission across the country by helping other nonprofits and for-profit firms enhance the independence, well-being and security of older people. And we returned home with new ideas that strengthened the company.

The beauty of Seniority has been to take the best of ABHOW, to share it and expand it, all to fulfill and sustain the mission. We learned, as many in our profession have learned, that the mission thrives when we pursue excellence in business practices.

We've been able to venture this way because we've had the full support of ABHOW President and CEO Dave Ferguson, another one of my mentors. His support points to another lesson, also learned by colleagues elsewhere: It is critical for senior leaders to lift the banner and raise the bar for purpose *and* professionalism.

From Seniority's startup through today, Dave has backed the enterprise and shaped it with his own significant expertise. He believes in this work. Since belief is what this book is all about, I ought to define the word now.

Belief is conviction that shapes action. Beliefs are not abstract propositions. Not feel-good thoughts. Not values that we merely hang in picture frames in community lobbies. Beliefs are roll-up-the-sleeves commitments, relentlessly pursued promises.

Belief always impacts what we do. There's no separating theory and practice here. Like mission and margin, or purpose and professionalism, belief and action go hand in hand. Genuine belief results in action. If there's no action, there's really no belief. Or, as the Christian scripture puts it, "Faith without works is dead."

Before I conclude this introduction, I want to share some of our vision, because it colors the chapters that follow. And the vision, like our history, also points to changes in our profession.

First and foremost, Seniority will continue to serve ABHOW. Seniority is ABHOW. We are a wholly owned subsidiary of ABHOW. We value ABHOW's heritage, and we seek to embody the company's core ethical principles. Our mission statement is the same as ABHOW's: "to enhance the independence, well-being and security of older people through the provision of housing, health care and supportive services."

We are grateful that this organization affords us the chance to pursue such meaningful work. And so our first commitment is to ensure that ABHOW receives our finest services. We fulfill this commitment by giving great attention to the particular needs and opportunities of ABHOW communities.

But there is another way we fulfill this commitment: by working with communities and organizations beyond ABHOW. Our contracts generate revenue for ABHOW while protecting ABHOW's tax-exempt status. Moreover, we develop programs for clients at minimal cost yet great value to ABHOW communities.

We head out into the senior living landscape as scouts for ABHOW, exploring new paths for the delivery of ABHOW's mission. What we discover is of great value to the organization. We take the best practices of third-party clients and incorporate them into ABHOW. We bring new knowledge into the ABHOW system about emerging products, such as equity-based communities, and innovative approaches, such as phased development.

In many respects, we are the company's R&D department – exploring, tinkering, inventing. This work of discovery is essential to the growth of ABHOW, as it is for any senior living organization that intends to thrive.

We are, for instance, helping ABHOW define its relationship to the Middle Tier – that market whose needs and income lie somewhere between affordable housing and continuing care. Through the development and management of multilevel rental retirement communities, we create products and services that enable ABHOW to serve another segment of the senior population. So as an arm of ABHOW that pursues new possibilities, we give the organization greater reach. In the next decade, we aim to reach far.

Today, Seniority is getting the "crème" of referrals. Banks and investment firms look to us as a proven resource for assistance with their clients for startup developments and crisis situations. They refer us to their clients because we are known for our ability to implement systems that lead to success.

My vision is to build on this reputation: to cultivate these referral sources, to leverage the confidence others place in us in order to grow both our management business and our sales and marketing contracts.

Throughout our contracts, we want the focus to be on partnership. We're not in it for the short term. We recognize that our systems take time to implement, that our methods require disciplined engagement day in and day out for months, even years. So while we often make recommendations that should be implemented immediately, we must also educate our clients to their long-term needs and cultivate a "gerontological patience." The long view is essential in this business of aging.

Fundamentally, we are partners for life, committed to personal, professional and organizational growth. We want our clients to regard us as essential members of their teams who are in it for the long haul, colleagues who can be counted on year after year.

Partnership signals another shift in our profession. We witnessed an explosion of industry vendors over the past two decades. Those business relationships have deepened so, and become such an ingrained part of the structure of our profession, that we speak more now of partnership. Today, for instance, architectural firms and technology companies are as much a part of the profession as "providers."

As long-term partners with our customers, training is at the heart of Seniority's work. We continually seek to strengthen our own capacity and the skills of our clients. We offer more than 80 sales training modules. We will continue to refine these tools to meet present needs, and we will look for opportunities to capitalize on the value of our training expertise and methodologies.

The discipline of training means we regard ourselves as a learning organization. If we are good scouts for ABHOW, then we are constantly gathering new data, taking note of trends, looking ahead for signs of change, and feeding this information back into the system. What makes us valuable consultants is not our certainty but our curiosity. The same could be said of the best leaders in our profession: They are always curious, always learning.

Seniority's learning leads to "practical innovation," which is a way of describing advances that can be implemented in any community. By being curious, by closely observing our clients and our processes, we're able to make modifications that may, for instance, turn around a troubled community, transition dining to an efficient and elegant experience, or transform CNAs and receptionists into marketing pros.

Moreover, "practical innovation" defines a way of engagement for us. It's a non-linear way of being consultants and managers: we notice, we tinker, we communicate. We constantly cycle through these stages. That's why you will always hear me preach the power of systems, which provide sets of practices that guide, chart, and communicate our progress toward success.

In the next few years, I see us becoming more adept at moving around this circle, more confident in the efficacy of our approach, and more invitational to others: we want people to learn with us. That means we will have to redouble our efforts to document our steps and to communicate with our clients. We never want our partners to be without the information they need to measure the outcomes of our management agreements or the success of our sales and marketing contracts.

Outcomes and measurement – that's another sign of change in our profession. Across senior living there is greater emphasis on tracking resident health and satisfaction. Health care reform as well as competition demands that we identify outcomes and assess progress. Our industry is measuring team member satisfaction, consumer awareness, and brand identification. In short, we are much more astute about metrics.

Partnering. Learning. Measuring our efforts. All of this is about the maturing of senior living. And all of this comes into play in Seniority Spirit, our hospitality and culture formation program. You'll read more about this initiative in the pages that follow. It's the most exciting facet of our company's work today – and it points to the enormous potential of our profession.

Since launching Seniority Spirit in 2009, I have noticed renewed enthusiasm among our team members. We believe more deeply and passionately. Daily we are recommitting ourselves to this work. The success of our team members in forming cultures built on exceptional service inspires me to dream anew about our firm's future as well as the future of senior living.

Here's the dream that fires my imagination:

I see a company where the team members are thrilled to be engaged in the work. I see a company in which our excitement and exceptional service so overwhelms our clients, our residents and their families that they cannot stop talking about the value of our firm. I imagine a company that fosters raving team members and raving customers. Is there a more beautiful picture of our future?

This is my vision for Seniority. It springs from my deep respect for the people of this company and my belief in our potential. I also believe in the potential of our profession. And so my vision for Seniority is also my hope for colleagues everywhere. The future of senior living will be shaped by all of us, by our convictions. And those convictions will be sustained by what we value.

So here is what I value:

I care about seniors. I believe we enrich the lives of older adults by offering them the opportunity to move into our communities.

I care about family. I look across our company and our profession and see people who genuinely care for each other. Our residents and their loved ones, our team members and our partners – we all comprise a family. And being family is where "the magic" happens. I have often said, "Family is laughing and crying (hopefully more tears of joy than not) and eating a lot of cake along the way!"

I care about building a business with quality products and strong systems. I value using best practices that increase our productivity in order to maximize the time to be face to face with our residents, team members and families.

I care about making a difference. My personal mission in life is service, and my desire is to serve in a manner that embodies these values.

The beauty of Seniority is that here I have such an opportunity, every day.

Wherever you are, you have such an opportunity as well.

PART ONE

CULTIVATING CONVICTION

"When you believe a thing,
believe it implicitly and unquestionably."
— *Walt Disney*

1.

YOU'VE GOT TO HAVE FAITH

The senior living profession faces a crisis of confidence. One challenge after another has confronted the industry since 2008: declines in occupancy, slower sales process, tighter capital markets, and now government reductions in Medicare and Medicaid reimbursement rates. The challenges are taking a toll on our profession. Leaders are anxious and exhausted, uncertainty hovers over many communities,

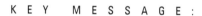

KEY MESSAGE:

Success in senior living depends on conviction that shapes action.

and our optimism about the future of senior living has dimmed. Most troubling of all, however, is that these challenges have revealed an unpleasant truth. Pushed by circumstances to the core of our beliefs about this work, some of us are coming up empty. The reason: We don't fully value our products and services.

This lack of conviction does not bode well for the future of senior living. Our success depends on confidence in our communities; our future hinges on the faith that our products and services make a difference. We know that dedicated professionals in many places share our concern. We want to sound the alarm, but more importantly we want to encourage the committed and motivate the uncertain.

We've got to have faith in senior living. Many of us profess belief in the principles of senior living – the commitments to create safe and compassionate communities and to honor the independence, self-determination and dignity of older adults. But belief in the abstract is not sufficient. It must be embodied in practice.

Can our profession overcome this crisis of confidence? We believe we can.

Self-Doubt in Senior Living

Every senior living leader is familiar with the reasons why we struggle mightily to sell our communities today. Slow home sales are hampering prospective residents. People are nervous about investing when the economy is so uncertain. Our customers are taking a wait-and-see approach. The reasons sound reasonable, and they may be valid. But is there more to the story?

Most senior living leaders would agree that tough times have eroded confidence in our profession. The Great Recession and the slow recovery have tempered our future forecasts, which were so optimistic just a few years ago. Our enthusiasm, built on the promise of aging baby boomers, has dimmed as reports show that many in this generation lack the financial wherewithal to retire.

More than ever before, leaders are openly expressing doubts about the long-term viability of the entrance fee-based model. Some organizations are moving quickly to introduce new entrance fee arrangements, including fully rebateable contracts, which begs the question, Will our industry be able to sustain the refund liability introduced over the last decade? All of the maneuvering on agreements has the feel of desperation, and the multiple options may even have the effect of confusing and turning away customers.

Most troubling of all is the reality that our profession's confidence was low even before the economic downturn. For some leaders, sales staff and community team members, there is a kind of self-doubt in senior living that few admit, a degree of embarrassment about our work, particularly in skilled nursing. For years many of us have extolled the virtues of our communities while privately saying, "I would never move here." Some of us might soften that position by saying we would make the move but only to a special community – one that hasn't been built yet. Either way, the statements reveal a disturbing truth about our profession, our dirty little secret: We don't fully value our products and services.

This lack of conviction does not bode well for our future, especially given present circumstances. Consumers, buffeted by fierce economic winds, are turning toward other options. State and federal governments, desperate to cut expenses and pay down debt, are reducing reimbursement rates because they know the public will not rise up in defense of nursing homes. Would *we* rise up? Could senior living leaders offer a genuine, confident, passionate defense of our profession?

The Necessity of Belief

To succeed we must truly believe in the value of our communities. Other industries understand how essential belief is. Southwest employees believe theirs is the best commercial airline in the U.S. Ritz-Carlton team members believe they have the power to create peak experiences for guests. Disney cast members believe in the magic. At Seniority we have always said, "You can't preach until you're baptized," which means our sales and our service must be rooted in conviction about the value of senior living. Belief is central to healthy culture formation, effective management, sales success and service excellence. The path to success is paved with confidence in our products and services.

For these reasons we are paying attention to the power of belief in our company and the wider profession. Through Seniority Spirit, our groundbreaking hospitality and culture formation initiative, it has become abundantly clear that belief fuels our every effort to deliver exceptional service. So we are keen to discover how belief arises and how it is cultivated among our team members and across our communities.

We define belief as *conviction that shapes action*. There is confidence in this conviction. You hear it in our Seniority Spirit motto: "We are exceptional people providing exceptional care and services." This is neither hype nor hyperbole. We are not trying to convince ourselves of the quality of our work. And this is not merely a feel-good effort. This is about the success of our business.

Our goals require belief. We aim to deliver on our commitment to create one-of-a-kind positive experiences for our residents and families. We want to deliver on our promise to clients, which is to build enduring relationships that are based upon mutual respect and integrity. And we seek to honor our team members by supporting creativity, compassion, positive attitude, respect and teamwork, all to encourage individual growth and maximum potential. We have to believe to succeed.

We must believe in each other, and we must believe in the value of our products and services. Our people must believe they create communities where residents not only enjoy newfound freedom but flourish. Our nursing staff must believe their care improves quality of life. Our sales teams, which face very real challenges every day, need to believe they can achieve 100 percent occupancy. Our success, then, depends on conviction that shapes action.

What We Believe

Imagine saying with pride, "I'm a chef at a retirement community," or "I manage a skilled nursing facility." Imagine telling an older adult in all sincerity, "You'll never regret moving here," or, to an adult child, saying with the utmost confidence, "Your mother will thrive here, which means you can reclaim the role of a daughter, not your mother's caregiver." We say these things at Seniority because they are true. And because these statements are true, we believe in our work, which means we have great faith in our communities.

Our team members, and our colleagues elsewhere who lead from conviction, know the value of our profession. Indeed, we share a common set of beliefs:

1. **We believe in the purpose of senior living.** In the U.S. and around the world, senior living communities play an essential role in meeting the needs of older adults and their families.

2. **We believe in the value of senior living.** Residents and their families enjoy the predictability of costs plus greater freedom, security and peace of mind when they choose our communities.

3. **We believe that mission drives everything.** Across our profession, mission is the motivator to serve. And mission should guide our every action.

4. **We believe in creating communities with our customers.** Our profession's future shines brightest in those places where our desire to serve complements our customers' desire to choose and to shape their own future.

5. **We believe in excellence.** We know we have the ability to create exceptional experiences for our customers, so we believe that excellence is always within our reach. Yet we also know that excellence is not a goal obtained but a path pursued. As Aristotle said, "We are what we repeatedly do. Excellence, then, is not an act, but a habit."

All five of these beliefs are essential to success in senior living. And the beliefs apply to all team members. However, if your community is struggling with a crisis of confidence, make sure that at least one group of team members is full of faith: your sales team. Sales leaders must be true believers. They are your evangelists, spreading the good news in your market and stirring up belief within your community.

If belief is lacking in your sales team, your customers will know. They can pick up on doubt and insincerity, says Seniority Vice President Joy Nance. "If the sales team doesn't believe in what they are selling, it is plain and simple: occupancy decreases and the back door opens widely," Nance says. "People who visit can quickly recognize your genuine care and concern for them personally. Conversely, your insincerity is even more recognizable when it comes to selling something you don't believe in."

Why We Believe

What is the basis for our belief in the value of senior living? In our profession *seeing is believing*. Senior living professionals who lead from conviction know the value of their communities because they see that value every day in the positive impact on residents and their families.

"You see the peace of mind in new residents' faces," says Seniority Vice President Teri Conklin, who has worked in senior living for nearly 20 years. "The stress from their lives is reduced or gone, they are laughing and meeting new friends. And the best reward of all is when a resident or an adult child comes back to the salesperson and says, 'I wish I would have done this sooner. This is the best decision I could have made.'"

Resident satisfaction surveys confirm this positive impact, as do the testimonials of adult children. But witnessing firsthand the difference our communities make is what really grounds our belief and reinforces it over time.

Seeing is believing, and the inverse is true, too: *Believing is seeing*.

Belief sharpens our vision, bringing into focus the customer right in front of us. Because we believe, because we are confident about the value of our community, we are freed of the anxiety of persuading a customer. Instead, we can truly pay attention to the customer and help that prospective resident make a decision that is best for him or her.

Moreover, belief inspires imagination. We can easily imagine how beneficial our communities will be to residents and their families.

We know research shows that older adults in retirement communities live longer, happier and healthier lives; and because our experience confirms the research, we can imagine that others will benefit, too. That conviction, then, fuels every presentation to prospective residents and every sales call. It couldn't be otherwise, for just as the Christian apostles said of their witness of good news, "We cannot help but speak of what we have seen and heard."[1]

Finally, belief shapes our vision for the future of senior living. At Seniority we are optimistic about the viability of the CCRC and lifecare models. Looking ahead, we see the ongoing need for campuses built around a continuum of care, and we see a market that will continue to choose this product. Yet this is not wishful thinking.

Consider our present situation. Residential occupancy declined in many parts of the U.S. during the downturn, but occupancy is now inching upward in certain markets. The decline was due, in part, to the delay of prospective residents in selling their homes or their reluctance to invest while their financial portfolios weakened. During this time, communities experienced an increase in average age at admission, given the financial environment and the introduction of services and products that enable frailer residents to stay in their homes. Increased entry age, not surprisingly, led to increased attrition. It was, as they say, the perfect storm.

The good news amid all this is that sales are up in many places, so the sales system is not broken. Indeed, this sales success shows that CCRCs and lifecare communities will continue to attract a portion of the market. Unfortunately, for many operators, sales have not outpaced attrition. Thus, the challenge is to stay ahead of attrition or, more specifically, make our communities appealing to younger customers.

There is more good news along these lines. We are seeing an increase in "greenfield" sales – developments in markets that were previously not served. Prospective residents make a future commitment, grounded in the sound belief that their homes will increase in value while their community is being built. That kind of savvy strategizing is characteristic of the generation that is now the focus of senior living marketing, the roughly 40 million-strong "silent generation," which is between the ages of 66-86. Without a doubt, this is the most ideal cohort for the CCRC and lifecare models.

This generation is rational and analytical. They are accustomed to doing a cost-benefit analysis for every transaction. So it is not hard for them to see the value of a CCRC or lifecare community. It's like an insurance policy, as LeadingAge CEO Larry Minnix puts it. "If I were to pick a list of risk-mitigating things seniors can put their money in," Minnix says, "this would be at the top of it because it provides them a place to live and levels of care for the rest of their life …"[2]

That logic makes sense to this generation – good news for CCRCs and lifecare communities.

One member of this cohort, a CCRC resident since 2005, put it this way to the New York Times: "When my wife and I decided to move into a CCRC, just before Christmas, we told each of our six children that our decision represented the most significant gift we had ever given them. Never will they experience the gut-wrenching anxiety of trying to figure out what to do with us. We are in a safe place now. No matter what the future brings, we can receive the level of end-of-life care that we needed." And to his generational peers, he offered this advice: "Don't burden your children with your elderly care. They will be anxious and troubled enough as they walk with you to the end."[3]

The Dynamics of Belief in Sales and Service

"Any company trying to compete … must figure out a way to engage the mind of nearly every employee," says Jack Welch, former CEO of General Electric. We would tweak that statement: Companies must find a way to engage the hearts *and* minds of *every* employee. In other words, we have to build our enterprises upon belief. Why? We see three reasons:

1. Belief engages employees.

Belief brings the whole person into the business. When we ask team members to serve with passion we are asking them to be fully present – to show up with belief in themselves and confidence in our products and services. We want team members to bring their highest values and aspirations to work every day. The permission to believe coupled with reinforcement of belief hooks team members, and it shows. "We tell people we love our job," says Marge Pope, a Seniority sales director at The Terraces of Phoenix. "They say, 'It's so obvious.'"

What we are describing is "employee engagement," a hot topic in business for more than a decade. *The Gallup Research Organization popularized the term in the 1990s.* Gallup's researchers define employee engagement as "the ability to capture the heads, hearts, and souls of your employees to instill an intrinsic desire and passion for excellence. Engaged employees want their organization to succeed because they feel connected emotionally, socially, and even spiritually to its mission, vision, and purpose."[4]

Gallup has demonstrated that engaged employees contribute significantly to the bottom line. At the same time, Gallup's research shows that less than 30 percent of employees are truly engaged. For that reason, employee engagement is "what every company wants, but few get," as author Tony Schwartz says.[5]

We want fully engaged team members at Seniority, and we are committed to shaping a culture where full engagement is the expectation. To do this we start with belief on the first day of employment.

At Day One orientation the conversation focuses on belief – what our new team members believe and what our company believes. We baptize these new team members into Seniority Spirit, which is the attitude, behavior and standards enabling us to provide exceptional service and positive experiences to our residents, team members and clients. Orientation continues through Day Two, Day 21 and Day 365, with support in between via the Daily Huddle and frequent coaching. It's a catechism of sorts: We begin with the tenets of our belief and keep digging deeper into the implications of belief, reinforcing why we believe and what difference our convictions make.

2. Belief engages customers.

Genuine belief is attractive to prospective residents and their families. Because the senior living sales process is fraught with anxiety, the customer is drawn to a salesperson who is not anxious. What puts the customer's mind at ease is a salesperson who is confident. That salesperson becomes a still point amid the chaos and confusing array of choices that confronts the customer.

Furthermore, belief engages prospective residents because their entire decision-making process is rooted in belief. Our customers are attempting to act on their own values and aspirations.

The decision to move to a senior living community is a higher-level activity when considered in light of Abraham Maslow's hierarchy of needs. Maslow's framework begins with basic physiological needs – food, water, and shelter – then moves upward to safety needs, social needs, esteem needs, and finally to that apex which is about the need to make sense of one's life, to flourish as a person, to be whole – "self-actualization," Maslow called it.

The senior living experience, while addressing basic needs, really encompasses these higher needs. Therefore, it is incumbent upon the salesperson to engage the customer at this higher level. When that happens, when a salesperson understands the significance of the sell, the customer moves from "shopping around" to full engagement.

3. Belief connects employees and customers in relationships of trust.

When engaged employees meet engaged customers, magic occurs.

Indeed, when belief is operative in the sales process, we move from skepticism on the part of the customer and persuasion on the part of the salesperson to genuine connection. That's a relationship built on trust.

Stephen Covey says we have an "innate propensity" to trust. In other words, we're predisposed to believe. Even in those situations where our doubts would naturally be highest – the used car lot, for instance – we are ready to put aside doubt and believe. We hold out hope that the salesperson will be trustworthy. We yearn for the experience to be positive. That we yearn is itself a sign of belief: We believe our yearning might be answered.

Consider how much further we can get on belief. If a customer is predisposed to believe, the customer will travel far with a salesperson. If the salesperson genuinely believes in his or her product, and believes that it can truly benefit the customer, he or she will go far with the customer. In this light the sales process is a mutually beneficial experience; it moves toward the satisfaction of each participant's needs and aspirations. Moreover, the quality of belief expedites the process. That's what Stephen Covey means by "the speed of trust."[6]

Relationships of trust begin with belief, and they grow as confidence increases. Our beliefs, those convictions that shape action, demonstrate integrity and thus establish and reinforce trust – between sales teams and customers, between management and frontline employees, between members of a team. And trust makes all the difference in our work. Indeed, we cannot succeed without it.

That's why Covey calls trust-building "the key leadership competency of the new global economy."[7] He writes, "Trust brings out the best in people and literally changes the dynamics of interaction. While it is true that a few abuse this trust, the vast, vast majority of people do not abuse it, but respond amazingly well to it. And when they do, they don't need external supervision, control, or the 'carrot and stick' approach to motivation. They are inspired. They run with the trust they were extended."[8]

Encouraging Belief

How do you cultivate belief in a senior living organization? We recommend the following five steps:

1. Hire true believers.

Passion-driven team members make all the difference. Passionate people are fully engaged advocates for the value of your community. True believers want to give great service because they find that doing so is fulfilling. Indeed, that's the reason the Ritz-Carlton does not provide cash rewards for good service. "(W)e don't think that money sponsors the kind of behavior we're looking for," says one Ritz-Carlton leader. "We believe ladies and gentlemen should be making each guest's stay memorable because they want to do that, not because they get compensated for doing that."[9]

When hiring new team members, Seniority looks for true believers who possess the following characteristics:

- **Passion for older adults.** We look for people who cannot imagine a more interesting market to serve. We want people who are curious about the lives of older adults. We hire people who are sensitive to the challenges of aging yet also open to great possibilities.

- **Commitment to excellence.** We look for people who are zealous about aiming high, people whose spirits soar when we raise the bar on performance.

- **Balance.** We look for people who can stand at the end of the day and savor the quality of the work completed that day. To do so requires balance, which is the marriage of drive and gratitude.

2. Form a believing culture.

Confidence is catching. So how do you unleash belief? Again, we say at Seniority "You can't preach until you're baptized." We want all our team members to be immersed in experiences of the community. We encourage team members to eat a meal in the dining room, work out in the fitness center, and have coffee with residents just to get to know them. Someone who has experienced the quality of the community will naturally believe more strongly in the value of the community. For that reason we make sure team members have authentic experiences of their campuses.

At Seniority we understand that a believing culture is a celebrating culture – an environment where even the smallest wins are recognized. So we celebrate often. Every day begins with a Daily Huddle, where we provide education and inspiration to team members plus celebrate with a "Stellar Story," an example of a colleague who made a difference.

And how do you engage team members across an organization in expressing and deepening belief when personnel, financial, service and physical plant challenges confront the community? Such challenges, while they are a concern, do not have to hinder belief. "At the end of the day, we're not selling the granite countertop," says Roberta Godden, a Seniority regional sales manager. "We're selling the peace of mind, lifestyle, and the security of the community – and that doesn't change. Even communities that are in redevelopment communicate 'we're in this together.'"

3. Practice belief.

It's one thing to say we believe. It's another to walk the talk. First and foremost, practicing belief means keeping our word. "Unlike a lot of businesses, we live with our customer," says Godden. "We're going to see them everyday. So it's important to us that we keep our word."

Godden says she knows when people really believe: They are the ones who practice listening. "Tour, brochure, door is the method some of our competitors use, but our people make the sales process very personal," Godden says. "We listen to the person first and find out what's important to them."

The fact that our salespeople do not rush to the pitch underscores belief in our products and services. Indeed, after listening intently to the prospect and understanding their needs and aspirations, we may recommend that the person go elsewhere. That's confidence. "This goes back to integrity," Godden says. "It's not just about filling apartments. We want to make sure this is a good fit."

4. Create disciples for quality.

True believers always want to make things better. Because they see value in the present product, they also see potential. So they want to work toward improvement – what St. Paul called "the most excellent way."[10]

For this reason, those who are charged with selling a product or delivering a service must have a hand in shaping it. Salespeople have something to say about the product of the future. Housekeeping team members have ideas about how to strengthen their workflow. Ask them. In doing so, you will show confidence in your team members' thinking and skill and, thereby, deepen their belief.

5. Share the good news.

We want to be evangelical about the value of senior living. That means being passionate advocates, true believers who aren't shy about connecting prospects with any part of the community.

Godden recalls a recent sales process in one of our communities. A couple from out of town responded to a direct mailing, and they needed education about how a CCRC works plus information about lifestyle opportunities for them in the community and the wider area. The sales counselor listened to the couple's concerns, then she proceeded to arrange for meetings with just about every department on campus. Moreover, the sales counselor facilitated conversations with residents, who, without coaching, validated everything the sales counselor had been saying about the value of the community. "It's a real example of walking the talk," Godden says.

What's most striking in this example is that the sales counselor's convictions shaped her actions. She could have operated on fear rather than belief – fear of revealing too much information, fear of introducing the prospective residents to other team members outside marketing, fear of what other residents would say about life in the community. Instead, she believed.

She had faith in the power of her community – and that made all the difference.

D I S C U S S I O N   Q U E S T I O N S

▮ What are your highest values and aspirations?

▮ What does your organization believe about senior living?

▮ Does your board, leadership and sales team truly believe in the value of your product?

▮ Will you move into your community? Would you recommend that your mother move into your community?

▮ To what extent do you show up with all that you believe? What prevents you from being fully engaged?

▮ How would you assess team member engagement in your organization?

▮ What concrete steps can you begin to take today to make clearer your beliefs and your organization's beliefs? What support will you need from your colleagues?

2.

GRANDPAS ROCK AND GRANDMAS ROLL

If your senior living organization has been around for a while, dig into your old advertising files and you'll discover some strange artifacts. The photo of Bingo night or shuffleboard. The shot of a nurse holding the hand of a frail yet smiling resident. Ad copy that's all about taking it easy, resting – hence, "Rest Home."

Well, it's not your grandma's retirement anymore.

{

KEY MESSAGE:

The work of senior living is about reinvention.

}

That was certainly clear in 1997 when we launched Seniority. However, although we knew a new type of senior was arriving at our doors, old habits and old stereotypes were hard to break. We had to keep putting in front of our clients, and each other, a strikingly different image of seniors: Grandpas rock and grandmas roll.

And the learning curve was not just about imagery. We had to realize that everything about our profession was changing. *Everything.* Whether it's seniors reframing their lives or retirement communities repositioning their campuses, the work of senior living is really about reinvention, which is an ongoing process.

One of Seniority's early projects was producing the award-winning documentary "Surfing for Life," which tells the story of legendary surfers who continue to catch the waves in their later years. With every ride, these surfers blow through our outdated understandings of old. But they are not trying to be young. Rather they are being who they are – surfers no matter their age – which means they're doing it their way. That's what makes their reinvention so refreshing.

In many ways our profession has been trying to catch up with these pioneering older adults. We've been talking about our "changing industry" since the 1990s, but three shifts seem particularly pronounced now.

First of all, the leaders of older retirement communities, campuses built more than 25 years ago, are well aware that reinvention is a requirement to thrive in today's market. We have moved beyond the rhetorical discussion of how communities will someday need to change for a new generation and all the speculation about consumer tastes and expectations. That day is here.

Furthermore, we've reached the "tipping point" in terms of awareness and action: a significant number of leaders are asking different questions. Now the conversation is very practical: How to reposition a mature community in a very competitive market? How to finance redevelopment? How to address the needs of current residents while redeveloping a campus?

The second shift has to do with sales and marketing. When Seniority started in 1997, much of our work was educating clients about the necessity of sales and marketing. Back then, many senior living providers had a passive approach to sales, reflected by the avoidance of that very word, and so our work in some places was quite elementary. "Can we all say SALES?"

Today, most communities have moved past that discomfort and resistance. The shift that's now occurring is the systematizing of sales and marketing. Increasingly, our clients understand how critical it is to strengthen the processes of lead generation, lead tracking, prospect cultivation, and closing the sale. We notice that more senior living executives believe their entire community shares the responsibility for sales and marketing. Consequently, they are budgeting for ongoing training.

A systematic approach is key to management success, too – a reality that more organizations recognize. That's the third shift: senior living providers are letting go of the fascination with the latest management fad and getting down to the hard but ultimately rewarding work of implementing proven systems. Practice, discipline, and a relentless attention to detail – these are the qualities that lead to success whether a community is in startup mode or a turnaround situation.

In our management contracts, our expert operators clearly communicate to staff the expectations about systems and the goals we seek to achieve. And then we roll up our sleeves to implement these systems, day in and day out. The results include deficiency-free operations, stronger financial performance, and satisfied customers.

These three shifts excite us at Seniority. And the readiness of our clients to embrace change is good news for our profession. It means many of us are thinking creatively about how we fulfill our missions. In other words, we are leading.

So take some satisfaction in this reality as you, too, reflect on your efforts. Celebrate the difference your work makes. Be encouraged by the big steps all of us are taking.

We are creating communities worthy of the reinventors of aging.

■ How are these three shifts – the repositioning of older communities, the systematizing of sales and marketing, and the attention to management disciplines – impacting your organization?

■ How much of your work reflects a compassionate business model, and how much is based in "That's the way we've always done it"?

■ What practices and operational standards are essential to sustain reinvention?

3.

GET IN THE HUDDLE

A curious sight draws in people passing by the Seniority offices. Every morning a small group of leaders stand in a circle. At first glance, it may look like an emergency, or it could be a party. It's not the former, but it does have the spirit of the latter: it's our Daily Huddle, an inspiring 15-minute meeting that starts each day.

> KEY MESSAGE:
>
> A brief standup meeting helps team members start each day with enthusiasm and a shared sense of purpose.

Across our managed sales offices and client communities, Seniority teams huddle to make announcements, share a common education topic, recognize significant milestones and team member success, and reinforce our culture. In the space of a few minutes, we remind each other how we make a difference in the lives of older adults and their families through service excellence. And then we head out to deliver on that promise.

The Daily Huddle is an important part of Seniority Spirit, our hospitality and culture formation initiative. Seniority Spirit reflects our distinct understanding of the management principles that drive team member empowerment and, ultimately, customer engagement and loyalty.

What excites me most is that Seniority Spirit is unique to our profession. We took 18 months to develop the program. We initially partnered with Ritz-Carlton – the undisputed leader in customer service – to learn details about hospitality. But then we designed our program specifically for our industry. Seniority Spirit is about creating a new culture in senior living communities. Our approach encompasses the attitudes, behaviors and standards that enable us to provide exceptional service and positive experiences to our residents, team members and clients.

The Daily Huddle is where we get to reinforce service excellence. There's always an educational component, which is an opportunity to bring people up to speed on topics like regulations and trends. We take a few moments to reacquaint ourselves with foundational documents, such as the mission statement or one of our 14 commitments to service excellence. We check in briefly on daily activities, such as resident moves. We celebrate team member achievement, then we close with an inspiring quote.

After only a few weeks, I became a big believer in the Daily Huddle. It doesn't take too much time or too much leadership. Indeed, leadership is shared as facilitation rotates among participants. And the outcome is clear: team members start the day with enthusiasm, motivated by a common purpose.

I look forward to our Daily Huddle, and I notice others do, too. At Cottonwood Court in Fresno, Calif., team members have embraced the practice. Executive Director Jim Stacy says the Daily Huddle has become the primary communication tool for his staff. Team members enjoy being exposed to other departments, and they welcome the regular reminder that they are all accountable to each other.

Jim Stacy notes one extra benefit of the Daily Huddle. It helps with marketing. The community puts its "best foot forward" each day because team members use the Daily Huddle to announce the day's tours and visitors. The result is that everyone is informed, motivated, and prepared to provide exceptional service.

I can't think of a better way to start the day.

DISCUSSION QUESTIONS

▪ How would you and your colleagues like to start each day?

▪ What commitments need to be reinforced daily? What successes?

▪ How can you ensure that all three shifts are consistently grounded in the leadership vision and mission?

4.

WATCH YOUR LANGUAGE

Would you rather live in a "unit" or an "apartment"? How about a "facility" or a "community"?

Without a doubt, most of us would choose the apartment in a community. A unit would turn us cold. A facility would just plain scare us.

Words matter. They repel and they attract. Obviously, we in the senior living profession must be mindful of the words we use. Grandmother's instruction is still relevant: "Watch your language."

> **KEY MESSAGE:**
> ## The words you use can make a positive impression on residents and guests.

That wisdom hasn't always been so obvious in senior living. When we launched Seniority in 1997, one of the first things we did was introduce our clients to a new lexicon. At the top of the bad word list: facility. Our founder, Joe Anderson, would fine us $1 every time we said the f-word. We quickly learned to watch our language!

Other words needed changing. "Unit" became apartment." "Admissions" changed to "move-ins." And "admissions directors" were now "sales and marketing directors."

We weren't the only ones making these changes. The language shift was and is a sign of the growing sophistication of our profession ("profession," not "industry"). Think about how far we've come. It wasn't long ago that only a brave or crazy few even whispered the word "sales" in senior living. Sales was a dirty word, remember? It was certainly not appropriate for mission-focused communities – so the thinking went.

Well, our profession has learned a lot in the past two decades. We know now that instead of being a necessary evil, sales is really a good and natural process of sharing a product or service we actually believe in. And being a "senior living sales professional" is truly a meaningful vocation – because we make such a difference in the lives of seniors and their families.

As we get savvier about sales, we continue to make changes in our language. We recognize that the use of language is one of the ways we can make a positive impression on residents and guests (not "patients" and "prospects," mind you). Our goal always is to use language that puts our communities in their best light and describes an atmosphere that is warm, caring, and homelike.

So we have to be vigilant, like Joe with his $1 fines. Even today, leaders can easily fall into the old language, especially without an intentional, collective effort to communicate in new ways. That's why we talk about language in our Seniority team member orientation and Daily Huddle.

We have to remind each other that certain words, such as "facility," "unit," "elderly," "admission," "discharge," "cafeteria," and "dementia care," will generally elicit negative associations.

Let's just agree – it's time to drop such words from our professional vocabulary.

Our grandmothers had one more bit of advice here: "Don't talk that way to each other." *Those* are words to live and work by.

DISCUSSION QUESTIONS

■ What words make a positive impression at your community?

■ What words make a negative impression at your community?

■ What measures have you taken to ensure that your communication is consistent with all team members? What additional steps can you take?

PART TWO

PRACTICING HOSPITALITY

"If there is any concept worth restoring to its original
depth and evocative potential, it is the concept of hospitality."

— *Henri Nouwen*

5.

GETTING REAL ABOUT HOSPITALITY

Enter the grand lobby and a concierge stands to greets you. She is the first in a line of guest relations staff whose sole purpose is to provide you with impeccable service. She draws your attention to the club-level experience that awaits you: the day spa to relax, the business center to work; multiple dining options, including a Starbucks, cocktail lounge, and elegant restaurant; and limousine service should you need to run an errand or want a night on the town.

It's all very "hotel-like" in this retirement community.

> KEY MESSAGE:
>
> ## Without a shift in culture, hospitality measures will be merely cosmetic or episodic.

A growing number of retirement communities are emulating the hospitality industry. Beginning in the 1980s, retirement communities started emphasizing hotel-like services and amenities. That trend accelerated when hoteliers Marriott and Hyatt entered the senior living business. Both companies trumpeted their hospitality background as a distinct advantage in attracting consumers looking for a different style of retirement living.

Over the past decade, the upscale hotel or resort has set the standard for design and service for retirement communities that aspire to excellence. "Yesterday's senior living communities often resembled hospitals," notes one journalist. "Tomorrow's will take their cues from hotels."[11] New luxury retirement communities promise to make residents "feel like they're in a five-star hotel," as one developer puts it.[12]

These are signs of a widely recognized trend in senior living. Yet senior living leaders generally have not fully explored the meaning of hospitality. In the narrowest sense, hospitality for retirement communities is about mimicking the practices that make high-end hotels so pleasurable for guests. In the larger sense, hospitality means creating a shared vision of service that satisfies both residents and employees.

That larger sense drives Seniority's interest in this topic. Our company defines hospitality as the "attitude, behavior and the standards enabling us to provide exceptional service and positive experiences to our residents, team members and clients." We call this Seniority Spirit. For us, as for other senior living leaders who embrace a larger view of hospitality, our work is about culture formation. Without a shift in culture – which is the common vision, corporate personality, and shared habits of a community – hospitality measures will be merely cosmetic or episodic.

We learn from the hospitality industry, of course. Indeed, we have spent considerable time studying with the best – with leaders of the Ritz-Carlton, in particular. But ultimately our task is to create a culture that honors what we know to be true, and best, about our service in the senior living field. So our hospitality motto is very specific to our profession: "Exceptional people providing exceptional care and services."

Furthermore, our aim is to have a model that can be incorporated into several locations with various types of senior care options: for-profit, nonprofit, CCRC, Lifecare, rental communities, and free-standing assisted living and memory support programs. So our big question is, How to do culture formation on this scale?

We understand that an approach like Ritz-Carlton's, while inspiring, cannot be overlaid on our industry, namely because our residents live with us while a hotelier aims for repeat customers in settings with an ever-revolving door. So our hospitality program is customized for residents and prospective residents. We recognize that sustainability is a critical issue if we are to avoid "training-of-the-month syndrome." For that reason, we have put in place supportive structures and systems to ensure that our approach to hospitality sticks. Finally, knowing that our communities operate on narrow margins, we have created a cost-effective program.

Like a growing number of our peers in this profession, we have embraced the change called for by an authentic approach to hospitality. The shift to hospitality signals our industry's growing sophistication and market orientation. The shift represents, in part, the continuing effort to redefine the retirement community, which has long struggled with negative public perceptions.

But hospitality also presents an opportunity to move well beyond marketing to a certain quality of experience. The energy that senior living leaders invest in this issue marks the difference between *hospitality as style* and *hospitality as substance*. For leaders who want to realize the full potential of hospitality, several challenges must be addressed. But first, let's review how we got here.

A Short History of Hospitality in Senior Living

The shift to hospitality is part of the continuing evolution of a product that traces its history in the U.S. back to the Civil War, when "homes for the aged" served widows and the frail elderly.

There were few changes in this model until the mid-20th century.

Small rest homes, board and care homes, and larger institutional settings were similar: they "took care of" older adults who had few resources in those years.

Not until after World War II did older adults have greater financial freedom through Social Security and pensions. The market responded to this middle-income consumer by offering different senior living products.

In 1949, our parent company, ABHOW, opened Pilgrim Haven in Los Altos, Calif. Pilgrim Haven became one of the nation's first continuing care retirement communities, offering multiple levels of living on one campus. The CCRC model spread in the 1950s and 1960s as older adults saw a wise investment: the freedom from household maintenance plus the security of on-site health care should they ever need it. At the same time, leisure communities, with resort-style offerings for the more affluent, began to emerge. Think Del Webb. His first retirement community, Sun City, opened outside Phoenix in 1960.

Through the 1970s and 1980s there were further signs of a shift to hospitality. Inspired by hotel architecture, major entrances and grand lobbies appeared in new retirement communities. Higher levels of service were offered. Dining became more elegant. A resident of one community recalls that in 1980 they used paper napkins, plastic cups and placemats. By the late 1980s, linen tablecloths and formal dining ware were standard. Increasingly, older adults were attracted to the lifestyle they could enjoy at a retirement community. Nonprofit and for-profit companies responded by building residences "that combine the convenience of a hotel with the community spirit of summer camp," as the New York Times put it in 1988.[13]

The entry of Marriott and Hyatt hastened the move to hospitality. The growth of these two senior living brands in the 1990s raised the stakes for traditional nonprofit providers of senior housing and health care. Nonprofits responded by emphasizing their mission-driven value while working mightily to mimic the more luxurious services and style of the newcomers.

During this same period, reconsideration of the design and service delivery of skilled nursing care sparked a national movement. Proponents argued for a social model of care rather than the entrenched medical model. They decried the "hospital-like" quarters and clinical feel of nursing homes. They envisioned residents living in smaller "households," where they would receive more person-centered care. This trend, which continues in the present under the banner of "culture change," intersects with the shift toward hospitality. Yet in culture change the accent is placed on *creating home*, a phrase that offers another way of defining hospitality in the senior living context.

Finally, interest in hospitality grew across the 1990s as senior living leaders contemplated the "coming age wave" – the 78 million baby boomers who began turning 65 in 2011. Everyone agreed that boomers would reject the old senior living models; new kinds of communities would have to be created.

Much was written on this "future shock." Researchers said the new older adults would hold vastly different views of retirement than their elders. Community living would appeal to some boomers, but these consumers would have significantly different tastes and expectations: they would expect larger apartments, want more flexibility in pricing and service packages, and be interested in entirely different programs that reflect new perspectives on aging.

Whole conferences were devoted to imagining the boomer retirement community. It would be culturally hip – California leaders envisioned the "Purple Haze Retirement Community." It might be university-based. It could be resort-like. It would definitely be full of freedom – with multiple dining options, lots of a la carte service offerings, plenty of gourmet coffee and blazing high-speed Internet access.

Inspired by this future, providers and developers moved quickly in the new millennium to build communities and remake old ones. Advertising featured more youthful and active customers, while "hotel-like" became a preferred description.

The motivations are mixed in the move to hospitality. At our best, the senior living profession wants to provide the highest level of service and is compelled by mission to seek out new approaches. At our worst, we may find in hospitality an avenue, ironically, to flee from aging. So the trend calls for greater reflection and examination in the light of mission. To move from *style* to *substance* in hospitality, senior living communities must contend with three challenges: the culture challenge, the customer challenge, and the leadership challenge.

The Culture Challenge

Historically, retirement communities have been built on the concept of "taking care" of the resident. While today's communities are less institutional, and "culture change" initiatives have cultivated a social rather than medical model, the idea of "taking care" of the resident persists. Hospitality offers the possibility of true culture change, but it requires much more than the notion of "pampering" the resident with resort-style services. Indeed, a recent survey of luxury hotel guests found that they want to be "excited" and "inspired" rather than pampered.[14]

Hospitality at its best creates the conditions for customers to have "wow" experiences. At Seniority, we call these experiences "Stellar Stories" – exciting and inspiring moments that shape and express a customer's personal identity.

Like any organization, a retirement community has a culture. That culture is the community's common vision and its corporate personality, its shared rituals and cherished habits. A culture shifts when its members take an active role in realizing the experiences they desire.

"Resident engagement" is the term used in senior living to describe this active role. Seniority Chairman Dave Ferguson says resident engagement means "moving away from 'taking care' of people to providing opportunities for personal growth and fulfillment." Noting that a philosophical shift is underway in senior living, Ferguson says,

> Many of our organizations were founded to preserve the dignity of residents. Although the goal is noble, sometimes our actions may seem patronizing. That's the unintentional shadow side of "taking care" of others.
>
> We are learning that the preservation of dignity is really about self-determination. This is true whether a resident is fully in-dependent or requires 24-hour nursing care. Expressing wishes, exercising the right to choose, shaping the life that is theirs – these are the practices of self-determination. We honor the dignity of others when we acknowledge their power.[15]

To be hospitable is to truly welcome the self-determination of residents. Hospitality in this sense means to make room for residents to have the experiences they seek. Resident engagement can take the form of participation in governance, leadership in programs, and decision-making that affects the shape of community life. Of necessity, resident engagement requires owners and staff to let go of some control.

The culture challenges are really multiple, then. How to loosen control in a highly regulated environment while maintaining quality and safety? How to move beyond "taking care" when health concerns are a reality? How to transform the team member's role from delivering goods or services to helping to create the conditions in which residents have memorable experiences? Answering these questions requires us to radically rethink the purpose of the retirement community. Everything must be on the table.

At Seniority, we examined our entire team member structure, from job descriptions to hiring practices to orientation to performance evaluation and ongoing training; and we looked critically at all of our resident programs. If our aim is to support residents in aging successfully, then our real work is to create environments where people thrive. That calls for a different mindset among team members who want to "take care" of others. Although seemingly noble, "taking care" gets in the way of flourishing. To embrace the latter, we need places that are truly hospitable. Obviously, that's a major culture shift for senior living.

The Customer Challenge

"Hotel-like" works for a certain group of affluent, highly independent consumers. Senior living's primary market today is the Silent generation, which is accustomed to the style of the hospitality industry. Many of these consumers are professionals who have spent their lives traveling, enjoying fine-dining, and expecting exceptional service. As healthy and independent residents, their presence is felt in senior living communities.

But the customer challenge is to recognize that senior living communities will continue to serve residents with diverse needs. Assisted living and memory support will likely see the most growth in the coming years. Some argue that the trend toward frailer residents will intensify, as baby boomers put off moving to retirement communities until their later years.

Along with these frailer residents, communities will welcome a growing number of residents who want the security of care, should they need it down the road, but for now regard the community as a base to re-engage the world on their terms, whether that means continued employment, volunteer work, travel or college studies.

The contrast in these converging populations is most evident in communities where repositioning or redevelopment is underway. Here we find a great variety of needs and expectations regarding services and amenities.

Current residents have lived with traditional service packages (e.g. three meals a day) and tried-and-true "comfort activities" such as the four Bs: Bible, bridge, bingo and birthdays. New residents, on the other hand, expect more flexible service packages (e.g. a spend-down account similar to country clubs) and activities that are more about life enrichment than passing the time. Subcultures may emerge – and clash. A community may communicate tension more than anything as it negotiates a new way amid an old environment.

But great strides can be made in the customer challenge by affirming one basic truth: Though residents are diverse, they and their families share a common desire: they seek experiences of excellence. Hospitality can be a response to this desire. The retirement community affirms the desire for meaningful and memorable experiences by saying to the consumer, "We will accompany you in this experience."

Moreover, hospitality can reshape that ironic mindset noted earlier – the anti-aging mentality sometimes at work in our profession. Yet to do so, hospitality must be more than "taking care" of frail residents or pampering the independent; rather it is about *being hospitable* – fully welcoming all residents, wherever they are in their life journey; providing holistic services that meet a range of needs and desires; and delivering all of these services with the highest degree of professionalism and the utmost respect for the dignity of residents. As the Ritz-Carlton motto puts it, "We are ladies and gentlemen serving ladies and gentlemen."

The Leadership Challenge

Leadership in a culture of hospitality is shared. In Seniority Spirit, the foundation of service is the same for every team member:

1. Greet everyone with a smile.

2. Anticipate, acknowledge and act.

3. Be warm and genuine.

Frontline employees are empowered to make decisions when a hospitality approach is fully implemented. One commitment that all Seniority team members make is the following: "I own every problem I see." The team member may not personally resolve every problem, but he or she *owns the responsibility* to ensure the problem is resolved – to find the right person, to communicate the need, to assist in any way possible.

Owning the responsibility comes naturally when there's a passion to serve. The passion to *take the lead* in delivering excellent service is palpable in a setting where hospitality is pursued. Shared leadership, then, requires a particular approach to management and a willingness and readiness on the part of team members to embrace their critical role.

Since ancient times, hospitality has been regarded as a matter of honor: respect accrues to the one who shows hospitality. The one who demonstrates hospitality, then, is not compelled by outside forces to be hospitable but is internally motivated to be hospitable. His or her own flourishing is bound up in treating the guest with dignity and graciousness. Companies that aim to deliver exceptional customer service understand this; these firms know that their employees want to deliver such service *because it fulfills them*. Thus, the leadership challenge is to recruit such special people, set the expectations for everyone, and train for excellence.

Meeting this challenge requires dedication to staff. Just as Seniority team members make a commitment, the company makes a commitment to them. Our Promise to the Team is the following:

At Seniority, our team members are the most important asset in providing exceptional service to our residents.

By supporting creativity, compassion, positive attitude, respect and teamwork, we encourage individual growth and maximum potential.

Seniority supports a work environment where diversity is embraced, family is valued and the Seniority Spirit is strengthened.

Toward Hospitality in Hard Times

Senior living leaders are challenged to move from style to substance in hospitality. And this challenge has come amid the worst economic downturn since the Great Depression. Yet, interestingly, the economic turmoil provides an opportunity to recast hospitality in its larger sense.

Hospitality as style can come with a high price tag. Conventional thinking has been that consumers will pay for the extra level of service. But there are doubts now about that assumption. Before the recession ended, researchers started forecasting a "post-recession consumer" who is cost-conscious, debt-averse, yet still interested in creating experiences, albeit experiences of simplicity. [16] If consumers are less interested in being pampered and they demand simplicity, *hospitality as style* will be less attractive. *Hospitality as substance*, on the other hand, will welcome the new frugality, make a home for it, and join with the consumer in recognizing there are more important things in life than luxury in itself.

Along those same lines, Eric Janszen writes,

> To win over newly tightfisted, debt-averse consumers, companies will need to follow the path of firms that succeeded in previous downturns by promoting value and utility over luxury and brand. Consumers won't be able to buy as many goods as before, but they'll react positively to marketing that allows them to feel their newfound thriftiness is a lifestyle choice rather than a constraint imposed by the economy. Messages that center on family, life simplification, and getting back to basics will appeal. [17]

Smart senior living leaders will understand that an exceptional experience is not contingent upon offering an upscale product or service; the exceptional experience can occur amid simplicity. While post-recession consumers are likely to retain habits of frugality, as human beings they will still yearn for meaningful experiences. Senior living communities have an opportunity to welcome – to be hospitable – to these desires.

▎What is your culture and who defines it?

▎How do your team members articulate this definition? What do their definitions say about your organization and the work ahead of you?

▎If you have multiple locations, is your culture consistent at each community or driven solely by the local executive director? What infrastructure would ensure culture consistency and sustainability?

▎What role do your customers play in shaping a culture of hospitality?

▎How are you defining leadership and to what extent are your team members embracing this definition?

▎How can you ensure that hospitality is not mere style but truly substantive in your organization?

6.

STARTING WITH A SMILE

The little things make all the difference in our profession. Take a smile, for instance. It costs nothing, but it changes everything. When it's absent, people notice. When it's there, it lights up the room.

But you already knew this, right? It's the sort of thing our grandmas taught us: Smile when you meet someone.

Because a smile is so basic, and so essential to delivering exceptional service, we've made it the centerpiece of Seniority Spirit. Greet everyone with a smile. That's our first Foundation of Service.

{
KEY MESSAGE:

Grandma's advice always applies: Smile when you meet someone.
}

Emphasizing the importance of smiling sounds so obvious, you might be thinking. But you also know this: Not everyone smiles.

How many times have you walked through a retail line where the cashier hardly acknowledges you? Why is the gruff "Next!" the first thing we often encounter? How is it that thousands upon thousands in retail and service industries have been trained to say "Can I help you?" but deliver that line with no trace of a smile?

We have a basic problem with customer service in America. Grandma's good advice hasn't stuck. But senior living is where we can turn this around, and what an appropriate place to begin: where our grandmas and grandpas are the customers.

Older generations value two things when it comes to customer service: a handshake and a smile. So that's where we start. Whenever passing a resident or prospect, every team member in our communities is instructed to make eye contact and smile.

We want our communities to be known as places where exceptional people provide exceptional care and services. We believe this goal is entirely within our reach.

It's doable for you, too. You simply have to start with a smile.

DISCUSSION QUESTIONS

▮ When was the last time you were greeted with a smile at a store or other business? How did that smile make you feel?

▮ Is smiling and eye contact practiced regularly by your team members?

▮ What gets in the way of smiling?

7.

OWNING EVERY PROBLEM

Walk around any senior living community, even the finest campus, and you're bound to find a few problems.

The front desk is a little messy. Chairs are askew in the dining room. A couple of flyers are out of date on the announcement board. If you don't see any problems, count on a few being presented to you on any given day. One resident's dishwasher is not working. Another resident wants to dispute a charge. The dining services staff is scrambling to cover the absence of several team members due to illness.

{

KEY MESSAGE:

You have control over how you respond to problems.

}

Is there such a thing as a problem-free community? Not in my experience. It's the nature of senior living campuses to always be faced with one challenge or another. Problems are an ever-present reality in such complex human enterprises. There's no way around it. But we do have control over how we respond to problems.

The famous shipbuilder Henry J. Kaiser once said, "Problems are only opportunities in work clothes." That perspective represents a significant shift in attitude. It signals a choice that is ours to make when faced with any problem.

At Seniority, our team members embrace this positive attitude. We claim the power of our choices amid challenges – and that posture inspires us. Indeed, this attitude is the heart of Seniority Spirit.

We expect all team members to make 14 commitments, one of which says, "I own every problem I see." Here's how that works:

If you're a dining services team member, and a resident tells you he locked himself out of his apartment, your job is to not pass this resident off to maintenance. Owning every problem means saying, "Mr. Smith, I am delighted to help you. I will ask our maintenance supervisor to meet you at your apartment immediately."

If you see litter on the campus, you never say, "That's buildings and grounds' job to pick up trash." Owning the problem means picking up the litter yourself. It's your campus, so you not only own the problem, you own the opportunity to make your campus as beautiful as possible.

This commitment to own every problem is so important to Seniority that we give team members permission to spend up to $250 to solve a problem. That sends a message to our customers – that we intend to deliver exceptional service.

And imagine what this commitment says to our team members. They hear loud and clear that we are exceptional people who have the power to create one-of-a-kind experiences for our customers. Claiming their power, team members want to step up. They discover that delivering exceptional service is inspiring and incredibly rewarding. So they're ready for any challenge.

Are you struggling to shift the attitude among your team members? Reframe the situation. It's not a problem. It's an opportunity!

DISCUSSION QUESTIONS

■ What is your response when you see a problem?

■ How do your fellow team members respond when confronted with problems – especially when the problems are "outside their area of responsibility"?

■ What's required to move beyond "areas of responsibility"? What can you do to empower team members to resolve issues independently?

8.

BRANDING IS RELATING

When advising our clients about the process of branding, we always emphasize that a brand is more than a logo. It's easy to focus on the logo – after all, branding goes back to burning a symbol on cattle. But brand means much more. Brand is about a relationship with the customer.

Think of Starbucks. Yes, the company has a recognizable logo, probably known more by its circular shape, green color and block type than the mermaid in the center. However, what people remember about Starbucks is the quality of the coffee and the experience of a Starbucks store.

{

KEY MESSAGE:

Brand is about a relationship with the customer.

}

They remember the ritual. It's the same every day, and customers expect that consistency. The experience is reassuring and reinforcing. Many people have to have their Starbucks. It's a relationship.

When brand is understood as relationship, two guiding principles stand out.

First, *pay attention to the customer.* That may seem obvious in a retirement community, where, in theory, the whole enterprise is about meeting the resident's needs. But paying attention is something more than delivering service: it means asking how the resident, or prospective resident, experiences the service. Is the experience consistent, every day, everywhere on campus? Is the customer satisfied with the experience?

Second, *remember that everything communicates.* The orderliness of the offices and the neatness of the gardens, the scent of the dining room and the sound in common spaces – it all communicates in a retirement community. The activity calendar and the art on the walls speak as loudly as the greeting at the front door.

As with any relationship, a brand takes time to build and time to maintain. The task is never complete. Even Starbucks, with its significant brand loyalty, has to be diligent about ongoing branding.

The good news is this task doesn't fall to just your sales and marketing team. That's one more thing we emphasize when consulting with our clients: Everyone shares in the work of branding – even customers.

Indeed, successful branding results in customers who clearly articulate what your community is about. They can talk about your brand because they have truly experienced it. They understand your brand because they have a relationship with you.

DISCUSSION QUESTIONS

■ How do your customers experience your brand? What do the sights and sounds of your organization say to customers?

■ When is your brand compromised?

■ What steps can your organization take to strengthen your brand and protect it?

PART THREE

KEEPING THE FAITH

"Success is not final, failure is not fatal; it is
the courage to continue that counts."

— *Winston Churchill*

9.

OUR ANGLE ON REPOSITIONING

I'm no prophet, but mark my words: Someone will talk about the baby boomers at your next senior living conference.

Surprised? I didn't think so. Our profession is awash with the news of the age wave.

Every conference and every publication draws attention to this coming tsunami. As the first of 78 million baby boomers turned 65 in 2011, the discussion only intensified. So we know all about these "new seniors" who will reject traditional notions of retirement. And we've heard all about the new communities built to suit them.

{
KEY MESSAGE:

The reimagining of a community's physical plant, services and brand requires a systematic approach – plus faith and realism.
}

But until now, little has been said about what to do with aging retirement communities, properties built 25 years ago and earlier to serve other generations. Beyond anecdotal information, we lack formal research into the practice of repositioning – the comprehensive reimagining of a community's physical plant, services, and brand.

We're working on this at Seniority. We are engaged in several repositioning processes with clients. And we're pausing to reflect on what it all means for the many mature campuses across the U.S. What we're finding is a need for a systematic approach to repositioning.

An Overview of Aging Communities

Leaders of older communities have been repeating a familiar refrain for some time: The next generation will want something different than what we currently offer.

"We are trying to de-institutionalize the building," said the CEO of a Virginia retirement community on the organization's $2.2 million overhaul of its skilled nursing center.[18]

"People will live longer and healthier lives if they stay active," noted the CEO of a Missouri community that spent $19 million to add a theater, art gallery, and sculpture garden to the campus, which was built in 1979.[19]

"Seniors are demanding more space," said the CEO of a century-old Wisconsin community when in the midst of a nearly $40 million expansion. "Years ago, it was very acceptable to walk down the hall for your shower. Today's seniors aren't willing to do that. And as we prepare for the baby boom, they aren't willing to do it either."[20]

Leaders of older retirement communities carry a double burden: the knowledge that America is aging *and* the recognition that their communities are not designed to respond. In 2011 the first of 78 million baby boomers began turning 65. Add to this mammoth cohort the reality that older generations – the G.I.'s and the Silents – are living longer, and you have a sense of the magnitude of an aging America. By 2030, when all baby boomers will be well into their mature years, one in five Americans will be over the age of 65 – an incredible increase compared to earlier years.[21]

Research tells us these new older adults will have vastly different views of retirement than their elders. Community living will continue to appeal to a portion of the population, but these consumers will have significantly different tastes and expectations than their predecessors. Because we senior living professionals have been immersed in this conversation for more than two decades, we can readily cite the differences: new consumers will expect larger apartments, want more flexibility in pricing and service packages, be interested in entirely different programs that reflect new perspectives on aging, and so on. Yes, we know: it's not our grandmother's retirement community anymore.

But how are established retirement communities to respond beyond mere cosmetic changes? Many communities were built for other generations. Sixty percent of skilled nursing facilities, 31 percent of residential living apartments, and a quarter of assisted living communities are 25 years or older in the nation's top 30 metro markets.[22] These communities are showing their age; alongside new product, older communities often look like relics from another era, conveying the "rest home" image they work so hard to shake.

So what to do? Renovating a community is a costly process, especially for a nonprofit organization with small margins. Considerable planning, creativity, and patience are required. Plus, leadership must find a way to balance future vision with present needs. The challenge of engaging current residents, and staff, in a plan for customers not yet here is immense. Some might wonder if it's worth all the effort.

Still, a growing number of communities are taking on the challenge of repositioning. They believe that such a move is consistent with the mission and crucial for survival. Between 2001-2005, repositioning accounted for the largest volume of financing activity by Ziegler Capital Market Groups – more than financing for new campuses, acquisition, and refinancing.[23] With median occupancy levels holding steady above 90 percent and cash flow improving, more communities will be willing to risk debt to reinvent themselves.

Repositioning – The Process of Rethinking Retirement Living

Leaders should consider three critical issues before embarking upon a repositioning process. The three issues are quite basic yet often receive scant attention. Certain assumptions about retirement living, for example, are treated as givens rather than critically engaged. Repositioning in its broadest sense is a process of rethinking retirement living. Before a hammer is lifted, we need to ask hard questions about a community's purpose, the market's needs and wishes, and where these two interests intersect.

1. Repositioning mature communities begins with an evaluation of assumptions regarding retirement living.

Why do older adults move to retirement communities? It's a fundamental question that leaders must wrestle with before commencing a repositioning process. Years ago, we assumed that older adults moved to retirement communities because they had a primary interest in community. So buildings were designed like dorms: small private rooms, larger common areas. And programs were developed with the group in mind, emphasizing the social connection that compelled older adults to choose congregate living.

Today, we assume that privacy is more important than community. Community is still a draw, but older adults want to enjoy their personal space – and they want plenty of it. This desire for personal space also shapes assumptions about service. Today's older adult wants personalized services and a variety of options. So the dining experience, for example, shifts from a single campus-wide approach with three meals a day (again, think dorm experience) to bistro style, offering several destinations on one campus with plenty of choices, and point-of-purchase flexibility.

Years ago, we emphasized that continuing care communities were places "you would never have to leave." The assumption was that older adults, above all, desired the assurance and security of a community that would be their home for the rest of their lives, even when their health needs changed. Today, while continuing to offer the assurance of care, we assume that older adults want to keep their options open. They will leave their apartment homes for several months to travel. Some want equity options, in the event they decide to sell and move elsewhere, and they want fully rebateable contracts. Others want rental options that don't lock them into long-term commitments. So we assume movement. That means communities have to be flexible.

This assumption relates to another: today's consumers want communities that support their active lifestyles. So they seek communities that are connected rather than an "escape" or a "retreat." The earlier assumption was that older adults wanted to "let go of it all" in retirement, find a quiet space away from the hubbub of life. Hence, the use of "haven" in many older retirement community names. But if movement marks senior living today, then a community will be connected to the wider community; its boundaries will be porous; it will see traffic and exchange as normal, and valuable.

This assumption has great implications for architecture, for services, and for marketing. Senior living leaders need to ask – "How do we bring the greater community into the walls of the retirement campus? And, how do we extend the campus into the greater community?"

2. Repositioning mature communities means wrestling with issues of space and design.

On the surface, this sounds obvious. But the conversation about space and design kicks up fundamental questions about purpose, mission, budget, stewardship of present resources, and responsiveness to the market.

We assume, for instance, that residents want larger homes. In Des Moines, Wash., we helped Judson Park Retirement Community, originally built in 1963, with a repositioning process that resulted in 64 new apartment homes with upwards of 1,250 square feet. The apartments have ample space for a fully equipped kitchen, washer and dryer, and master bedroom with a walk-in closet – a space considerably larger than the industry average for a two-bedroom apartment. Twenty years ago, small studio and one-bedroom apartments were the norm. Over the past two decades, many retirement communities have combined apartments here and there to create larger homes. A repositioning process, however, calls for a more thorough conversion.

But what if the site size is limited? How to get the most out of your site? Where space constraints are real, some communities will expand apartment size but lower the overall number of apartments. Financial and mission questions now arise. How do fewer apartments affect the bottom line? Will the fewer number of apartments be so expensive as to price them out of the market or the audience you have historically served?

Increasingly, we see interest in "building green," incorporating environmentally sensitive materials and practices into the design of a community. New consumers desire green spaces, organic gardens, protecting night sky, and energy-saving systems. While "building green" can lead to cost-savings over time, the approach requires a significant investment up front – in planning and dollars.

If we assume porous boundaries for the community of the future, how do resources in the greater community figure into the retirement community's redesign? For instance, can some spaces, experiences, or services be obtained beyond the walls of the retirement community? Could an adjacent fitness center co-brand its services with the retirement community? Does a nearby university become the setting for educational programming? Partnerships become all the more important now. The community of the future may be comprised of a network of relationships that deliver services to consumers.

Finally, how do you build so that the next big thing or change can be accommodated? Apart from the ability to convert assisted living space into, say, memory support, the industry is still years away from "flexible architecture" that makes entire senior living campuses malleable.

For that reason, repositioning is not a once every 25 years event; rather, the process must be a continuous function of operations in order to remain competitive and responsive to changing market demands.

3. Repositioning mature communities requires attending to the brand.

Talk of "brand" and "brand-building" is more prevalent in the senior living industry today, but often the term brand is narrowly defined as a community's name and logo. Brand is so much more. Brand is a community's identity, which is composed of its history, personality, and relationships with consumers. Some marketing experts speak of brand as a set of promises made by a company and understood by consumers; so a strong brand is one that keeps its promises.

The repositioning process is an opportunity to inquire into a community's brand. Some leaders mistakenly believe that repositioning is a chance to rewrite all the old associations with the community's brand. But if a brand includes history, promises, and present relationships, leaders will be sensitive to old associations and careful to reposition the brand with authenticity and integrity.

Nowhere is this challenge more pronounced than in the relationship with current residents. Promises have been made; associations and expectations are firmly embedded; the organization and the consumers share history. It is imperative that repositioning takes into account this present relationship.

Senior living professionals know that satisfied residents are the best marketing. Yet repositioning processes can easily slip into fascination with customers to come at the neglect of those already present. To avoid such a situation, leaders should be aware of critical issues with respect to current residents:

- *Resident input in redesign* – Residents naturally want a say in how their communities are remade. And the best processes will enroll residents at the outset so that they in turn become enthusiastic ambassadors for the redevelopment. Operations, however, must define the process, including the parameters within which residents give input and the communications that keep them informed and enrolled along the way.

- *Old agreements vs. new agreements* – New consumers desire numerous contract options. Yet communities must balance options with "confusion of the product." Proceed with caution here, and be sure legal counsel and marketing staff work closely on this one.

- *Pricing* – It's critical to be continually aware of the competition's pricing. Resident fees will generally bear the cost of new construction, so it's important to establish reasonable rates based upon the market and the added value of the redevelopment.

- *Relocation* – Once construction begins, current residents may need to be relocated. Community leaders can't communicate enough in advance of this change. Families should be kept in the loop as well. Here a "next generation" advisory group, comprised in part of family members, could play an important role.

The bottom line is that exceptional customer service becomes all the more important in a repositioning process. Strong internal communications are essential. Current residents must never be ignored. So the senior living leader becomes a communications expert, starting with the audience already present.

Alongside this internal emphasis is the need to reframe or rearticulate the community's brand to new consumers and other external audiences. Repositioning, as the term suggests, means a reintroduction of a community, perhaps as a different product with a different message. In many cases, we want consumers to make new associations with the brand; we want the market to hear new promises. In the branding of the new product we are mindful of the heritage and value of the original community *and* the opportunity to build new relationships with consumers who would not consider the older community.

But this is a delicate matter. A brand is not something to play with carelessly. So leaders must give thought to important questions of brand and branding. What is it that you want the brand to communicate? What does your brand already say? What changes in language are required? What new messages ring true, and which sound inauthentic? How long does it take to move the public to a new view of an old community? And finally, how do current residents become bearers of the new message?

A brand is a dynamic concept – always being formed, enhanced, and sometimes diminished by the matching of associations with reality and the keeping of (or failure to keep) promises. The dynamic quality of the brand may become more apparent in the repositioning process, especially when consumers are asked to believe in a product that doesn't yet exist, at least not fully. Prospects must be compelled to see the possibilities of the repositioned community. How do we do that when the idea is just conceptual, or when construction is underway? Quality, consistent external communications are critical.

Faithful Response, Realistic Assessment

"If you build it, they will come," was the mantra of the 1980s and 1990s, inspired by the courage – or craziness, depending upon your perspective – of an Iowa farmer who heeds a voice that tells him to build a baseball diamond in a cornfield. Today, there's no guarantee on future response to our repositioning initiatives. Getting ready for the next generation is a risky proposition. What if baby boomers change their minds and upend the expectations our industry has worked so hard to chart over the past two decades? Will we sink or swim in this coming age wave?

Good leadership takes faith, a willingness to venture amid unknowns. For leaders of mature retirement communities, repositioning is a faithful response to mission and a realistic assessment of the market and future possibilities. Repositioning, above all, is an opportunity to rethink the larger purposes of our communities and to reimagine retirement living. Wise leaders will take that journey, asking hard questions at the outset.

■ What assumptions about your product and your customers must you consider before embarking upon a repositioning project?

■ What's valuable about the older community that should be carried forward in the new campus?

■ What planning do you need to do to address the 'culture clash' between your current resident population and future residents moving into your master plan product?

■ How can current residents be enlisted as ambassadors of the repositioned community?

10.

A SYSTEMATIC APPROACH TO TACKLE TOUGH TIMES

In my travels across the country, I am struck by how hard senior living leaders are working to address occupancy issues and manage budgets in a difficult economy. Some markets and communities are struggling more than others, but what is common is the dedication: the willingness to work long hours, the rallying of teams to solve these problems, the stick-to-it-iveness. That commitment inspires me, as it does my colleagues in Seniority. We're motivated more than ever now to roll up our sleeves with clients and partners, to use all our skill and passion to make a difference in this profession.

> KEY MESSAGE:
>
> The key to success to success is marrying hard work with smart work, which means using systems.

The key to success, we believe, is marrying hard work with smart work. That combination is exemplified in the premium we place on systems, which are the practices and processes that ensure success in all facets of community life. Whether it's sales and marketing, health care, resident programming, dining or housekeeping, systems focus our efforts. They give us a consistent framework to guide our activities day in and day out, and they provide a mechanism to measure progress.

Budgeting systems are a good example – and particularly important to address right now. In our managed communities, we start with realistic budgets that support the programs and level of service we desire. The budgets must be attainable, otherwise service and quality of care decline. Plus, employee morale suffers when goals are out of reach. So we give our supervisors realistic budgets. We train them and support them in managing these budgets, and we hold them accountable. All along the way, systems are used.

We have standard hiring processes to make sure we get quality supervisors who understand the dynamics of expense control. Budget-building, formatting, and monitoring procedures are the same to ensure consistency and more easily track progress. We use training systems to teach budget management, and we provide ongoing support around the practice of budget reporting. Finally, budget management is a critical measure in performance review – another system – to ensure accountability.

Rather than being onerous, the systems actually boost confidence in budgeting, even amid tough times like these. Supervisors know and live by the fiscal management controls. We use computerized spend-down procedures when behind in budget in a certain month. Our executive directors conduct monthly audits and twice-monthly reviews of departments over budget. So the systems take the guesswork out of fiscal management. The practices relieve anxiety. Surprisingly, they even inspire us.

One last thing about systems: they are disciplines we share. They keep us working harder and smarter in cooperation with our colleagues. That means we get the benefit of mutual support and accountability, so critical in good times and bad. And when success comes, we get to celebrate – together.

DISCUSSION QUESTIONS

▌ What systems in your organization guide daily activities and help you measure progress?

▌ What systems require duplicative efforts or hinder your team members in other ways?

▌ How could your existing systems be enhanced? What new systems should be introduced? And how will you ensure compliance?

11.

Have you noticed how forgiving spring is? No matter our mistakes in previous seasons, spring always returns with life and beauty, plus opportunity: another chance to get it right.

{

K E Y   M E S S A G E :

A good cleanup of your sales office will bring clarity to the sales process.

}

For senior living sales professionals, spring is the season to get our houses in order. It's time to organize our sales systems, straighten up our marketing practices, and clear out the debris — all those distractions that keep us from generating leads, cultivating prospects, and closing sales. After several years of economic uncertainty and sluggish sales for many senior living communities, a deep cleaning is in order. It's time for *3-D spring cleaning*.

First, *de-clutter*.

A sales office can easily be overwhelmed by stuff: campus activities, staff meetings, volunteer assignments – stuff that has nothing to do with the sales process. This stuff is important for your community but not necessarily most important for you. Your job is to keep the community full so that others can do their jobs well.

De-cluttering means clearing your calendar of those activities that eat up your time and take you away from sales.

Second, *discard.*

A good spring-cleaning effort will always turn up things that you just don't need anymore. See that outworn shoe box system for prospect cards? Get rid of the cards and go to a web-based lead tracking system. Notice those boxes of old brochures that are missing the Equal Housing logo? Recycle them. You shouldn't be handing out these brochures anyway.

Discarding applies to old habits, too. For instance, it may be time to dump the old sales office schedule of 9 to 5 Monday-Friday and make yourself available when many consumers want to shop – in the evenings and on weekends. Consider spreading out your staff for six- or seven-day coverage plus evening hours. If your sales staff is limited, make sure that others in your community understand their marketing role.

Third, *discern.*

Once you've cleared the calendar of distractions and dumped that stuff you don't need, you'll see things in a new way. And clarity always sharpens the sales process. For example, you'll be able to take time to map out a sales call before you pick up the phone. What are you aiming for in this call? What objections might arise? And how will you respond?

Freed of distractions, you'll get to know your customers better. You'll see their lives more clearly, and you'll ask more perceptive questions, which are critical to closing the sale.

Indeed, you'll see yourself and your work more clearly. That's because discerning really means knowing what's most important for you to do – today, next month, next year. Spring graciously provides that annual opportunity to get our priorities straight.

DISCUSSION QUESTIONS

▌ What stuff is getting in the way of sales at your organization? What can you get rid of right away?

▌ Are your salespeople focused on revenue-generating activities or distracted by daily operations functions?

▌ Who reviews your monthly sales reports? How is feedback provided to your sales team?

12.

STICK BY YOUR GUNS

If you are a senior living sales professional, you know what may await you in the office today. News of attrition – now there are more apartments to fill. Hot prospects cooling off – so you've got to hustle for more leads. And budget warnings from top leadership – which means a lot rides on your performance.

Will you call in sick? Not likely. Most sales professionals don't run from challenge – that's why you're a professional. But even the best of us will sometimes let go of hard yet proven sales tactics in the hopes that another method will turn things around.

{
KEY MESSAGE:

Don't give into the pressure to abandon what you know works.
}

Hear that voice in the distance? That's me shouting, "Don't do it!" Don't quit. Don't give into the pressure to abandon what you know works. Around Seniority we have a rallying cry for just such moments:

Stick by your guns!

You know that success in sales depends in part on making a certain number of phone calls every day. There's no way around that. But senior living sales people will often jettison that task in favor of "building relationships." Stick by your guns! As good as "building relationships" sounds, this will generally take you further away from your primary task, which is to sell.

You know that the sales process is long and that it requires particular steps: appointments, follow-up at specific intervals, overcoming objections, and closing the sale. You have to manage your activity. Indeed, you know you have to be brutal about your schedule and disciplined about your habits. But sales people sometimes fool themselves into thinking that "creative brainstorming" or "talking strategy" is what they need to do. Don't do it! Stick by your guns! What your community most needs from you are sales. And, as the wise Walt Disney once said, "The way to get started is to quit talking and begin doing."

There's no sugarcoating the challenge you are up against as a senior living sales professional. This is a tough market, and it will only get tougher as new economic realities reshape consumer behavior and competition stiffens. But our work makes a difference. That means all our effort will ultimately pay off for our communities and the people we serve.

So don't quit. Roll up your sleeves, and pick up the phone. Keep working those tried-and-true sales systems. Stick by your guns.

DISCUSSION QUESTIONS

▌What sales systems are you tempted to let go of, and why?

▌What distracts you from those disciplines that work? Do you find yourself in operations meetings that exceed an hour in duration?

▌How can sales team members better support each other in the sales process? (For instance, how about a dedicated time each day when phone calls are the priority for the sales team?)

PART FOUR

ENGAGING THE FAITHFUL

"If I am going to be an authentic member of a team,
I'd like to know what's expected of me, and I'd really like to
have a leader ask me what I'm bringing to the game."

— *Max De Pree*

13.

CHANGE FOR EVERYONE

Change has never been so pronounced in senior living as it is today. Our communities are changing as customers change. Our business models are shifting in response to new economic realities. And everywhere there is talk of "culture change." The term itself is even subject to change. Some leaders use culture change to describe the shift to person-centered care. Others employ the phrase to describe the move toward more homelike design in care settings. Still others use culture change to advocate greater excellence in customer service. Whatever the definition, what's common is the belief that leaders drive culture change.

> **KEY MESSAGE:**
>
> You and your fellow team members shape a culture of hospitality as you discover that your own well-being is bound up in the service you offer others.

While leadership is crucial in culture change, not enough attention is paid to the role of employees. Ultimately, the formation of a healthy culture depends upon employees practicing certain habits day in and day out. In a senior living community, a healthy culture – and by "culture" we mean the attitudes, behaviors and standards that shape and reinforce action – emerges as employees discover that their own well-being is bound up in the hospitality they offer others.

One of the sources of confusion in senior living is the term "culture change" itself. As generally understood, the term suggests that culture change is something leaders make happen; and as the term relates to employees, the common understanding (or misunderstanding) is that leaders must change employees' attitudes and behaviors. But this is not how substantive and sustainable change occurs. Real change happens when employees themselves choose to alter their habits in order to realize greater fulfillment or satisfaction in their work. As former Herman Miller CEO Max De Pree puts it: "The organization can never be something that I as a member don't choose to be."[24] For that reason, "culture formation" is a more fitting term; it signifies the process of building upon employees' own strengths and aspirations.

A Story of How a Culture Is Formed

Not long ago one of our team members overheard a resident who was getting her hair done in the beauty salon say she wished someone would also apply her makeup. The team member didn't work in the beauty salon. She just happened to be there. Nevertheless, she took it upon herself to answer this resident's request. And the result was a very happy customer.

The story illustrates two important points. First, the team member took the initiative to serve the resident. She didn't run out of the beauty salon for fear of getting roped into a job that's "not hers." She didn't politely pass the request on to someone else. Instead, she paid attention to the resident, and she saw the resident's request through to completion. The second point: This is how a community's culture is formed – by small yet significant gestures of exceptional service. That means a single individual can help shape the culture, which we define as *the attitudes, behaviors and standards of an organization that guide and reinforce individual and collective action*. It didn't take long for the team member to apply the makeup, but her service made the resident's day. And it made the community shine.

"Culture change" is often presented as management-driven. But culture is truly formed at the front line as team members embrace the task to create one-of-a-kind experiences for residents. Fredda helped shape her culture by following through on one of the 14 service commitments that undergird Seniority Spirit, our hospitality and culture formation program introduced in December 2009: "I promptly respond to the needs and unexpressed wishes of our residents."

In this story the team member took the initiative and performed a task that is not listed on her job description but is consistent with her vocational aspiration: she wants to provide exceptional service. Had she not taken the initiative, she would have missed out on an experience that is important to her own well-being. As it happened, she followed her instinct, trusted her own desire to serve, and stepped out of her official role to apply the resident's makeup. She made a change, and that change marks the culture of her community.

The good feelings engendered by such an action – both the resident's delight and the team member's satisfaction in serving – contribute to the community's overall spirit, which is synonymous with culture. Such positive behavior becomes contagious. Imagine that kind of service, and the resulting delight and satisfaction, repeated across a community. The impact is really exponential. So one person can make a huge difference.

Later that day after her visit to the beauty salon, the resident came to the team member, took her hand, and said, "Thank you. I feel so beautiful. I feel like a queen!" The team member must have felt special, too. That's what happens when we offer exceptional service: we create cultures where everyone's joy is palpable. We all feel like royalty.

A Theory of Change

This story upends conventional wisdom about how change occurs.

Traditional thinking says that leadership, generally the top leader, must drive change. The "drive" metaphor is revealing: it suggests the leader is the operator of a machine (people) that won't move until the operator makes it move; or, to use the more "natural" metaphor, the leader is the herder of cattle (people) that must be pushed and prodded to go in a particular direction.

Two assumptions are implicit in this way of thinking:

1. People do not want to change.

2. The leader must make people change.

For leaders who seek to shape their cultures in lasting ways, it is important to unpack these two assumptions. The dominant thinking on leadership is built upon these assumptions. Most of the literature emphasizes how the leader *makes change happen*. The leader sets the vision. The leader mobilizes the followers. The leader gets people to behave in new ways and so produces change.[25] In this way of thinking, we could easily imagine that the leader's task becomes all the more important in a senior living community, where, we might assume, team members who are comfortable in old habits of serving older adults not only do not want to change but will actively resist change. So now everything really depends on the leader. But notice again the beauty salon story. No one told the team member to change. No one told her what to do. She took it upon herself to provide extra service to the resident *because she wanted to*.

Daniel Pink offers a different take on "drive." Rather than using it as the metaphor for the task of leaders, Pink locates "drive" within people. "Drive" is the intrinsic motivation people have to make their lives better, to find more meaning in their work, to improve their performance – to change.

Pink draws upon recent research as well as the work of Douglas McGregor, who in the late 1950s began to articulate a new understanding of intrinsic motivation. The conventional thinking, which McGregor called Theory X, was that "most people must be coerced, controlled, directed, and threatened with punishment to get them to put forth adequate effort toward the achievement of organizational objectives." But McGregor had another view, which he called Theory Y, that people actually want responsibility and are self-motivated.[26]

McGregor and Pink's perspective is borne out at Plymouth Village in Redlands, Calif., where Seniority manages the sales and marketing office. Recently, a couple made a deposit for an apartment home at the community, but soon after the husband died and the wife decided to delay the move. She asked for a refund of her deposit. The sales and marketing team went much further – on their own initiative. After talking with the wife about her food preferences, the team had a personal chef prepare three meals and delivered them to the wife. She and her family were blown away by the community's compassion and generosity. The experience was incredibly rewarding for our team members, too, because they want the responsibility to provide exceptional service and are motivated to attain this goal.

If people are self-motivated, then a leader's attempt to push and prod team members to change will at a minimum offend them or, worse, turn them off to the change the leader seeks. Those closest to the leader may buy in to his or her vision, but the impact is limited. Seth Kahan calls it the "lighthouse effect": where the leader is talking, the light is shining; but just outside the light things go dark quickly.[27]

True change happens not by imposition of the leader's values but through engagement that reveals shared values, Kahan says. For that reason, communication must be dialogical rather than one-way. Indeed, a vision of change might only truly emerge and be authentically received as people make meaning together, Kahan says. He references "social construction," the process whereby individuals make meaning via relationships and figure out things along the way rather than in advance.[28] So real change is something we do together, which means it is incumbent upon senior leaders to be in dialogue with frontline team members. And dialogue means listening.

There is one more element to add to this theory of change: People embrace the new only as they see the new preserving what's most important about the old. People change in order to honor some essential aspect of who they are. That paradox is at the heart of a self-organizing world. All creatures and living systems constantly seek change and organize themselves for change, but we only move toward a new situation by drawing upon who we have been, according to Margaret J. Wheatley and Myron Kellner-Rogers.[29]

We tap those habits and perceptions we have developed over time as we have made choices about who we will be. Scientists call this "self-reference," a kind of backward-looking process that, paradoxically, moves us forward. Wheatley and Kellner-Rogers write, "We will change our self if we believe that the change will preserve our self. We are unable to change if we cannot find ourselves in a new version of the world. We must be able to see that who we are will be available in this new situation."[30]

Consider a longtime CNA in a skilled nursing center, a team member whose habits have been formed over years of daily service and is now being told she must change her practices. Change is possible for her. Yet she will only change as she recognizes that the core of who she is – her genuine concern for residents, for example; or her natural gift for conversation – is preserved in the new situation.

Leaders who seek change, then, must be mindful of who their team members are and attuned to what is most important to them. Wheatley and Kellner-Rogers put it this way: "We encourage others to change only if we honor who they are now. We ourselves engage in change only as we discover that we might be more of who we are by becoming something different."[31]

We now have a three-part theory of change:

1. People have an inner drive to change.

2. People make sense of change and figure out the path of change in conversation with each other.

3. People change in order to preserve the core of who they are.

Start With What Team Members Want

At the first orientation session for new Seniority team members, we do an exercise called "Focus on You." We ask team members a series of questions: What makes you really happy? What is one of your strengths? What is the best part of working with seniors? And we ask them to name one benefit of great service. The activity is not just an icebreaker. We need to know what makes every team member tick and what they aspire to, because this is the path of passion and potential, the most sustainable way to truly shape a culture of exceptional service.

Team members want two seemingly contradictory things: autonomy and accountability. Daniel Pink notes the belief that autonomy is a "way to bypass accountability," but that's not true. Autonomy is not about Lone Ranger independence, Pink says. Rather it's about the power to exercise choice – for our own benefit as well as for others. So from the start autonomy has a relational or communal quality, a connection to others who would hold us accountable.

This framework needs a little more explanation. First, on autonomy. Team members want the freedom to exercise their power to make good choices. This desire is most apparent in the midst of problem situations. Through Seniority Spirit we have noticed that team members eagerly embrace the commitment to "own every problem I see." Here's how that works:

If you're a dining services team member, and a resident tells you he locked himself out of his apartment, your job is not to pass this resident off to maintenance. Owning every problem means saying, "Mr. Smith, I am delighted to help you. I will ask our maintenance supervisor to meet you at your apartment immediately."

If you see litter on the campus, you never say, "That's buildings and grounds' job to pick up trash." Owning the problem means picking up the litter yourself. It's your campus, so you not only own the problem, you own the opportunity to make your campus as beautiful as possible.

This commitment to own every problem is so important to Seniority that we give team members permission to spend up to $250 to solve a problem. That sends a message to our residents and their families: that we intend to deliver exceptional service. And imagine what this commitment says to our team members. It is an acknowledgement of the team members' power. They hear loud and clear that we are exceptional people who have the freedom and permission to create one-of-a-kind experiences for our customers.

Knowing that, and claiming their power, team members want to step up. They discover that delivering exceptional service is inspiring and incredibly rewarding. Recall the beauty salon story and other similar instances that happen every day in senior living communities. We offer simple gestures of hospitality – a helping hand, a little extra attention, a small kindness like applying a resident's makeup – not because these acts are required, though at times we may start the gesture out of a sense of duty; ultimately, we do this because we want the joy of the gesture. We discover that our own well-being is connected to the hospitality we offer others. The gesture of that team member in the beauty salon certainly impressed the resident, made her feel special, and truly made the resident's day. But that gesture also made the team member's day. In offering such hospitality, the team member gave herself the gift of joy.

Disney, perhaps more than any other hospitality or entertainment company, gets this. Why do their cast members go to such lengths to make their guests feel special? They do it because it makes them, the cast, feel special. Disney team members recognize they have the power of magic, and it charms them.

Similarly, our team members embrace the opportunity to serve, and they gladly take the initiative to serve. The encouragement to be autonomous is not regarded as burdensome but rather fulfillment of what they desire. Team members want to move toward mastery, which is the flourishing of their gifts freely exercised. "I feel more responsible knowing that I'm valued and at the same time knowing that everything I do counts," says one of our team members, a medical technician supervisor. "It makes me feel special."

But autonomy isn't the end. It goes hand in hand with accountability. Our desire for mastery is bound up in community. We want to exercise our power *and* we want our colleagues to respectfully remind us to use that power to fulfill our potential. That's why Max De Pree is keen to hear this question: "What are you going to bring in terms of competence, contributions, and commitment to this project?" De Pree adds, "I would gladly follow a leader who asks that kind of question."[32]

De Pree's comment underscores another lesson we have learned in Seniority Spirit. We do not have to compel people to work with each other. They want good working relationships because of the mutual benefit. One of our 14 commitments in Seniority Spirit is this: "I build meaningful relationships with those I work with and serve." Our experience tells us there is a direct correlation between the depth of team member relationships and the reach of our service. When relationships between team members are deep, when our trust is strong and we welcome mutual accountability, our capacity to serve is extended.

The mutual regard of meaningful relationships makes all the difference. The latest research shows that employee engagement comes about not because of carrots and sticks, nor through reward programs or punitive measures, but because of respect.[33] Team members want to know they are truly valued; and they want to work in environments where respect for everyone is abundant. To put it another way, team members want hospitality: communities that welcome their gifts and call out their potential.

Such respect makes Ritz-Carlton a star in the world of hospitality. The company's motto is rooted in mutual respect – self-respect plus respect for the other: "We are Ladies and Gentleman serving Ladies and Gentlemen." Inspired by Ritz-Carlton's holistic understanding of hospitality, we set about to develop our own approach for senior living; but our motto for Seniority Spirit is anchored in the same mutual respect: "We are exceptional people providing exceptional care and services."

So What Are Leaders For?

Our theory of change begs the question: If people have an inner drive to change, if they figure out change together and over time rather than via advance directives from the top, and if they change only as they see the core of who they are being preserved in the new situation, what then is the point of leadership?

We see four important tasks for senior leaders and managers:

1. Senior leaders and managers "set the table" for change.

2. Senior leaders and managers engage team members in constructing and interpreting change.

3. Senior leaders and managers encourage celebration on the way to change.

4. Senior leaders and managers carry the banner all the way.

All four tasks are critical. Our theory of change does not discount the role of leaders but rather suggests more crucial and effective practices for good leadership.

Setting the Table

For culture formation to succeed, every team member must understand why we're doing this, what's at stake, and how he or she plays such a critical role. Communicating this and engaging team members in conversation about the purpose of our effort is the work of leaders. It's the first order of business for hospitality. Call it "setting the table." That's why orientation for new team members is a centerpiece of Seniority Spirit. Here team members learn what we mean by exceptional service, and they discover how much power they have to shape the culture of their community.

Orientation occurs on the first two days of employment. Indeed, team members cannot work until they complete the two-day session. And we focus on culture rather than paperwork. When we launched Seniority Spirit in December 2009, all of our existing team members went through the two-day orientation. That means everyone in our company is grounded in the Foundation of Service and 14 Service Commitments that exemplify Seniority Spirit.

We talk about greeting everyone with a smile, about being warm and genuine. We underscore our commitment to own every problem we see, to build meaningful relationships with those we work with and serve, to be truthful in what we say and honest in what we do. These commitments should sound familiar. They are the kinds of lessons our grandmothers taught us. But we need the dedicated time of orientation to be reacquainted with this wisdom.

Our orientation doesn't end here. Every team member is assigned to a learning coach who helps the team member apply Seniority Spirit in daily tasks. Because it takes 21 days to make a habit, we don't certify team members until the Day 21 Orientation. At the 365-day mark, every team member goes through a half-day recertification session. All along the way, every day, our team members are immersed in Seniority Spirit through their Daily Huddle, a 15-minute standup meeting where they get education, information, and inspiration.

Why so much focus on orientation? It's plain and simple: successful culture formation depends on our team members. Our company's ambition to be known for exceptional service rests on team members behaving in certain ways, every day. So we want our team members to catch Seniority Spirit from day one. To do this effectively, and systematically, we need our leaders to set the table.

Engaging Team Members

Leaders engage team members in interpreting change. Recall Seth Kahan's comment on social construction: people make meaning together. When it comes to understanding change, people figure it out with each other, in conversation and in collaboration. One of the places where social construction occurs in Seniority is our Daily Huddle.

Across our managed sales offices and client communities, Seniority teams have a 15-minute meeting to start each day. Our teams use this standup meeting to make announcements, share a common education topic, recognize significant milestones and team member success, and reinforce our culture. In the space of a few minutes, we remind each other how we make a difference in the lives of older adults and their families through service excellence. And then we head out to deliver on that promise – to change things together.

The Daily Huddle is one important way that our team members learn. They learn because the Daily Huddle is always interactive and participative, with leadership of certain elements rotated among the team members. The Daily Huddle is social construction: together our teams figure out what change means in their communities.

It's interesting that leaders have known for years how important it is for people to be involved in their learning, indeed, that learning does not occur without their full participation. And we have known how positive people can be when they have a hand in making decisions that affect their lives. Notice, for instance, this piece of insight from 1945: "(A) person ceases to be reactive and contrary in respect to a desirable course of conduct only when he himself has had a hand in declaring that course of conduct to be desirable."[34] Yet we seem to keep reverting to a mechanistic understanding of leadership, treating people as parts that can be turned and tightened, aligned or replaced. No wonder, then, there is resistance to change when we forget that team members are human beings with needs, aspirations, and creative energy. But we can choose a different way, the better way of engagement. All we have to do is remember what we already know, and trust that knowledge.

Encouraging Celebration

Leaders occupy a symbolic role in the organization, which means team members will often look to leaders for cues about how to behave. So when leaders encourage celebration, they set the tone for others. Leaders signal that it is both good and essential to highlight achievement, recognize performance, and mark milestones.

Stellar Stories are one way we celebrate in Seniority. These short stories, which can be documented by anyone, capture moments when team members have provided exceptional service. Stellar Stories are shared in the Daily Huddle and in other forms in the community, and they are shared across our company.

When leaders encourage celebration, they acknowledge that the change we seek is indeed happening. Even the smallest acts of celebration – a note, a brief moment of recognition, a high-five in a hallway – reinforce what the effort is all about.

Carrying the Banner

Senior leaders and managers must articulate why all the effort of culture formation is worthwhile. This is the banner they carry. They communicate the purpose of culture formation at the outset, and they reinforce it all along the way. They fly this flag in meetings and in one-on-one supervision. When seemingly conflicting pressures compel team members to sideline hospitality, leaders must raise the banner even higher. At the end of the day, leaders' own behaviors will speak loudest. Leaders must consistently practice those habits they preach.

Staking Our Future on Team Members

At the very beginning of the first day of orientation for new Seniority team members, the facilitator makes an important statement: "*You* are the most important resource in providing exceptional care and services to our residents and their families!" We truly believe this. Indeed, we are staking our company's future on our team members.

For that reason, we underscore the role of team members in culture formation. We place the accent there because the emphasis is long overdue. Furthermore, we think it is time to issue a wake-up call to leaders who may be valiantly trying to "drive change" but finding themselves sputtering, stalling out or, worse, crashing. There is a role for senior leaders and managers in culture formation, which we have sketched out here. That role is not to "drive change," however, but to engage team members in shaping their work, their teams, and the spirit of their communities.

That said, the last word on the relationship between leaders and frontline team members in culture formation has not been written. All of us must pay attention to the interplay between senior leaders, managers and frontline team members – it is a dance, really, with noticeable patterns yet surprises as well. We must look for signs of success, drawing out the lessons and applying this knowledge to the improvement of our organizations.

As commitment to hospitality deepens in the senior living profession, we have the opportunity to practice hospitality all across our organizations; in other words, we can be hospitable not only to our residents but to each other. When we fully practice hospitality, we will form cultures that welcome everyone, that call everyone to their best, that become, in Max De Pree's wonderful phrase, "places of realized potential."[35]

DISCUSSION QUESTIONS

▌ Think about a change initiative in your organization. Were you able to sustain the desired change? If so, what factors contributed to your success? How critical was it for your team members to own the change?

▌ What are the key competencies that must be developed on your senior leadership team in order to "set the table" for your team members' success?

▌ What banner is senior leadership carrying? To what degree do your leaders' behaviors match the message of your banner?

▌ How much of your organization's orientation program defines culture and team member expectations? How do you continue orienting team members and reinforcing desired habits and behaviors?

▌ What are the signs of your team members' self-motivation? What additional responsibilities would they gladly take on? How might your team members' own passion shape the culture of your organization?

14.

ORIENTING FOR INSPIRATION

When was the last time you sat through your organization's orientation for new employees? What did you learn about your purpose and how did you experience your organization's passion? Were you inspired?

Probably not. We don't typically associate inspiration with orientation. There's information, of course. And paperwork, for sure. But orientation doesn't generally energize people. It's a procedure that leaders have to do and new employees must endure.

{
KEY MESSAGE :

Orientation is a critical process that calls for substantial organizational commitment.
}

Several years ago we decided that wasn't good enough for Seniority. We were curious about how to convey our culture. We were eager to train for customer service. And we wanted new team members to experience who we truly are as a company – to feel the spirit that informs our every action. We wanted new team members to be inspired.

So we turned orientation upside down. Rather than simply run through an employee handbook, we engage new team members in imagining how their talent will be leveraged. Instead of overwhelming – or really, underwhelming – new team members with a series of departmental presentations, we show them how their work will embody Seniority Spirit, which is the attitude, behavior and standards that enable us to provide exceptional service and positive experiences to our residents, team members and clients.

We still complete the paperwork and other requirements, but we spend the first two days of employment on our culture and hospitality training. Why? So that every new team member understands the expectations immediately, and everyone has the chance to say, "Yes, this is what I signed up for."

We've learned two important lessons after two years of reorienting orientation. First, the change requires substantial commitment on the part of the organization. There's a financial commitment, since no new team member begins without completing Day One and Day Two Orientation. And there's a time commitment for senior leadership, because we believe the message of exceptional service must come from the very top.

The second lesson, and the most important one, is that orientation is a process, not a one-time event. When our new team members complete Day One and Day Two, they are just getting started. At Day 21, team members share how they are living out our core commitments and they provide feedback on how we are living up to our promise to support them. At Day 365, we reinforce everything that has been taught and we celebrate one year of service.

On top of these sessions, team members receive ongoing support from a learning coach and continued grounding in our purpose via the Daily Huddle. Our purpose, we've concluded, calls for a sustained process of orientation. And our experience shows us the process makes a difference.

One new team member put it best: "I was so excited when I went through the training. I said, 'Thank you, God! This is the organization I've been looking for.' It really clicked for me."

That's the wow we want from orientation. That's inspiration!

DISCUSSION QUESTIONS

▌ What do your organization's team members take away from orientation besides paperwork? What do they learn about your culture?

▌ What would make your orientation more inspiring?

▌ What systems and training are needed to make your orientation meaningful?

15.

EMPLOYEE SATISFACTION = SUCCESS

It goes without saying, but I'll say it anyway: Employee satisfaction is critical to the success of a senior living community. The quality of the services we provide hinges on having employees who are passionate about the mission, happy in their jobs, and proud of their contributions.

{

KEY MESSAGE:

Satisfied team members are productive, innovative and motivated.

}

That may seem obvious. Yet too often we overlook the importance of employee satisfaction in senior living.

Resident satisfaction commands our attention, and rightly so. We want residents to be happy, feel secure, and enjoy peace of mind. After all, that's our mission. However, employee satisfaction is just as important.

Why? Satisfied employees are productive. They are innovative.

They own every problem they see. They are motivated to create one-of-a-kind positive experiences for residents and families because that's most fulfilling.

In other words, such employees know their own satisfaction is bound up with the customer's satisfaction.

That said, employee satisfaction is never easy to achieve, especially in difficult economic times when assorted anxieties tax our employees. It takes a lot of effort to achieve high satisfaction. We have to empower employees through shared goals and emphasize mutual accountability. We have to communicate clearly and regularly so that everyone understands what's expected. Plus we need to provide consistent recognition of success.

And we must do all of this every day.

When we do, there's magic – the kind of magic that delights everyone, perhaps team members most of all.

I can only imagine how excited our team members were at Courtside Cottages in Vacaville, Calif., one Christmas when a team member took it upon herself to create some magic.

While decorating for Christmas, the team member overheard a resident say she wished she could have a white Christmas like the ones she grew up with in South Dakota. That's all our team member needed to hear. She immediately went into magic-making mode and contacted a snow machine rental company, which donated the machine for a full week at a huge discount, provided free snow and threw in a sleigh. Another local business provided discounts on outside lights and décor. A church offered a nativity scene. And a family member played Santa. On a beautiful winter night in Northern California, the resident's dream of a white Christmas came true.

How would you and your team members feel if you took this kind of initiative and created such magic for your residents? My hunch is you would be thrilled – and you would want to do it again and again.

That's certainly true at Seniority. Our team members regularly express high satisfaction in opinion surveys because they are highly engaged. Overwhelmingly, they are proud to work for Seniority, and they believe they personally make a difference. They've got what we call Seniority Spirit – the attitude, behavior and standards enabling us to provide exceptional service.

Want to "wow" your residents and prospective residents? Satisfied employees are the key.

DISCUSSION QUESTIONS

▌ How satisfied are your organization's team members?

▌ What steps can your organization take to increase employee satisfaction and instill enthusiasm?

▌ Apart from surveys, how will you know that team members are satisfied? How can you measure and provide feedback regarding a team member's attitude?

16.

IF YOU QUIT, YOU MISS THE PARTY

To paraphrase Benjamin Franklin, in this world of senior living, nothing can be said to be certain, except death and regulations.

Success is never guaranteed. Indeed, with increasing competition, greater complexity in products and services, higher labor costs, high employee turnover, miniscule margins for Medicare, etc., etc., the business of senior living is just plain hard.

> KEY MESSAGE:
> ## Don't let up. Stick to it so you can celebrate.

It couldn't get any harder at Holly Creek a few years ago. Seniority was hired when pre-sales stalled during the critical period before finance and construction of this continuing care retirement community, located in Centennial, Colo. Faced with a monumental sales task, the organization's board started considering exit strategies.

But we wouldn't let up. We knew our systems would work if we worked them diligently. The result of our sticking with it was 100 percent occupancy for the community's first phase. Today our systems and people are proving their mettle again as Holly Creek's second phase is 98 percent reserved as of this month.

In the end, we work to celebrate. What a thrill it is to aim high and work hard. And what a joy it is to see our visions become reality: to witness communities literally rising from the dirt, to see residents excited about the adventure of retirement, to share with our colleagues the privilege of meaningful work and the satisfaction of a job well done.

But if you quit, you miss the party. Just ask Dejen Grebremeskel.

At the 2011 New Balance Indoor Grand Prix track meet in Boston, the Ethiopian runner lost a shoe at the start of the 3,000 meters. What happened next was remarkable.

While the TV commentators suggested it might be best for him to drop out, Gebremeskel kept running. With one shoe. For 14 laps.

His foot was in pain, he said in an interview afterward, "but I couldn't focus on that because I had to fight for whatever I could achieve."[36] In an inspiring display of determination, he passed his competitors and crossed the finish line in first. It was an exceptional performance driven by belief. "I'm so happy that I didn't quit, that I didn't lose," he said.

May we all be just as driven in senior living. We are racing toward a goal that matters: vibrant communities where the spirit soars. So let's keep reminding each other what the work is all about.

Let's encourage each other to have faith in the future of senior living. To be confident in the knowledge that our work makes a difference. To remember the passion that first brought us into this profession.

As the band Journey puts it, "Don't stop believin'. Hold on to the feelin'."

DISCUSSION QUESTIONS

▮ What stories can you and your colleagues tell each other about sticking with it?

▮ What do you want to celebrate 90 days from now? Six months from now? In a year?

NOTES

[1] Acts 4:20.

[2] From Fox Business News interview, August 2010.

[3] Quoted by Paula Span in "The Bright Side of CCRCs," *The New York Times*, The New Old Age Blog, http://newoldage.blogs. nytimes.com, Nov. 6, 2009.

[4] John H. Fleming and Jim Asplund, "Where Employee Engagement Happens," *Gallup Management Journal*, http://gmj. gallup.com, Nov. 8, 2007.

[5] Tony Schwartz, "What It Takes to Be a Great Employer," Harvard Business Review Blog Network, http://blogs.hbr.org, Jan. 3, 2011.

[6] Stephen M.R. Covey, *The Speed of Trust: The One Thing That Changes Everything* (New York, NY: Free Press, 2006).

[7] Ibid., 21.

[8] Ibid., 319.

[9] Jennifer Robinson, "How the Ritz-Carlton Is Reinventing Itself," *Gallup Management Journal*, http://gmj.gallup.com, Oct. 12, 2006.

[10] 1 Corinthians 12:31.

[11] Bob Moos, "Senior Communities Take Cues from Resorts," *The Dallas Morning News*, July 11, 2007.

[12] Sara Clemence, "Ritzy Retirement Communities," Forbes.com, Feb. 24, 2006.

[13] Robin Pogrebin, "Among the Elderly, Togetherness Is Selling," *The New York Times*, Aug. 28, 1988.

[14] Jonathan Barsky, "Luxury Hotels and Recession: A View from Around the World," white paper published by Market Metrix, May 2009, 7.

15 David B. Ferguson, "Resident Engagement Is the Future," *ABHOW E-News*, September 2007.

16 Paul Flatters and Michael Willmott, "Understanding the Post-Recession Consumer," *Harvard Business Review*, July-August 2009.

17 Eric Janszen, "Selling to the Debt-Averse Consumer," *Harvard Business Review*, July-August 2009, 113.

18 *The Roanoke (VA) Times*, Oct. 7, 1999.

19 *St. Louis Post-Dispatch*, Nov. 18, 2005.

20 JS Online, *Milwaukee Journal Sentinel*, Oct. 18, 2002.

21 Thirteen percent of the total population was 65 and older in 1997, 8.1 percent in 1950, and 4.1 percent in 1900, according to the Population Resource Center.

22 Statistics from Market Area Profiles (MAP), May 2006, National Investment Center for the Seniors Housing and Care Industry. Figures include freestanding, continuing care, and other multilevel living communities.

23 "Dramatic Repositionings in the Desert," a 2005 presentation by Ziegler Capital Market Groups.

24 Max De Pree, *Leading Without Power: Finding Hope in Serving Community* (San Francisco: Jossey-Bass, 1997), 105.

25 While John P. Kotter offers valuable insight on the need to connect with employees' emotions in any change effort, his take on the role of the leader is fairly conventional and an example of the dominant thinking: "Leadership *defines* what the future should look like, *aligns* people with that vision, and *inspires* them to make it happen despite the obstacles" [emphasis added]. His title says it all: *Leading Change* (Boston: Harvard Business School Press, 1996).

[26] Daniel Pink, *Drive: The Surprising Truth about What Motivates Us* (New York: Riverhead Books, 2009), 76.

[27] Seth Kahan, *Getting Change Right: How Leaders Transform Organizations from the Inside Out* (San Francisco: Jossey-Bass, 2010), 2ff.

[28] Ibid., 17-18.

[29] Margaret J. Wheatley and Myron Kellner-Rogers, *A Simpler Way* (San Francisco: Berrett-Koehler, 1999).

[30] Ibid., 50.

[31] Ibid.

[32] De Pree, 80.

[33] Paul L. Marciano, *Carrots and Sticks Don't Work: Build a Culture of Employee Engagement with the Principles of Respect* (New York: McGraw-Hill, 2010).

[34] Gordon W. Allport, "The Psychology of Participation," from *Selected Readings in Management*, ed. Fremont A. Shull, Jr. (Homewood, Ill.: Richard D. Irwin, Inc., 1958), 223. Allport's article was originally published in 1945 in *The Psychology Review*.

[35] De Pree, 105.

[36] Sabrina Yohannes, "A Brief Chat With Dejen Gebremeskel," *Runner's World*, http://racingnews.runnersworld.com, Feb. 8, 2011.

ABOUT THE AUTHORS

M. Sloan Bentley is president of Seniority, Inc., a senior living management, sales and marketing firm based in Pleasanton, Calif. She was one of the founding members of the company, which was formed in 1997. A gerontologist and licensed nursing home administrator, Ms. Bentley supports clients with a thorough understanding of the field and extensive experience in operations and marketing. Prior to joining Seniority, she served on both the corporate staff and as a community executive director for Northern California Presbyterian Homes. She is a skilled sales trainer and a highly regarded speaker for state and national organizations in senior housing and health care. Ms. Bentley earned her bachelor's degree in gerontology from Bowling Green State University and a master's in long-term care administration from the University of North Texas.

Daniel Pryfogle is principal and creative director of Signal Hill, a Cary, N.C.-based leadership and communications consultancy. Along with Ms. Bentley, he was one of the founding members of Seniority.

LEARN MORE

Do you want to deepen your organization's belief in senior living? Seniority offers educational presentations and facilitates board, senior leadership, and organization-wide explorations of the issues raised in this book. Call Seniority President Sloan Bentley at 925-924-7187 to learn more.

9961873R0008

Made in the USA
Charleston, SC
27 October 2011